AS History
UNIT 2

OCR

Module 2584: England, 1780–1846

Neil Whiskerd

Series Editor: Derrick Murphy

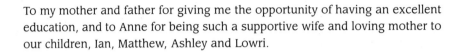

To my mother and father for giving me the opportunity of having an excellent education, and to Anne for being such a supportive wife and loving mother to our children, Ian, Matthew, Ashley and Lowri.

Philip Allan Updates
Market Place
Deddington
Oxfordshire
OX15 0SE

tel: 01869 338652
fax: 01869 337590
e-mail: sales@philipallan.co.uk
www.philipallan.co.uk

This Guide has been written specifically to support students preparing for the OCR History Unit 2 examination. The content has been neither approved nor endorsed by OCR and remains the sole responsibility of the author.

Typeset by Alden Bookset, Oxford
Printed by Information Press, Eynsham, Oxford

Contents

Introduction

Aims

This unit guide covers English history in the period 1780–1846. After studying Module 2584, students should have a good understanding of the various historical developments that occurred in this period. The specification for this option is divided into four study topics, namely:

(1) The age of Pitt and Liverpool, 1783–1830
(2) War and peace, 1793–1841
(3) The age of Peel, 1829–46
(4) The economy and industrialisation, 1780–1846

The key issues for each study topic are dealt with in the Content Guidance section, where advice is given on historical content and understanding. As regards assessment, the examination is 1 hour long, and candidates are required to choose one two-part structured question from a choice of four, each question relating to one of the four themes of this particular unit. If you are studying this unit for AS only, it is worth 30% of your overall assessment. If, however, you are studying the full A-level, this unit is worth 15% of your overall mark.

Many of the skills that you have acquired from your GCSE course will be very relevant when you begin the A-level course. There are, however, a number of new skills that you will learn during the first year of the course, such as evaluation and an ability to analyse different opinions from a variety of different angles. History is a literary subject and obviously those who are able to write in clear and concise English will have a distinct advantage over others who are less capable. There will be numerous opportunities throughout the year to improve your writing skills. The key skill to work on is essay writing under timed conditions. You will have some experience of this at GCSE, but you will need to refine these skills in your first year. This option relies solely on your ability to write two full and accurate essays in 1 hour.

- The first sub-question, worth 30 marks, requires you to explain or examine a certain issue arising from the key content of the unit you are studying.
- The second sub-question, usually on a separate area of the specification, is worth 60 marks and requires you to use higher-level skills such as evaluation, analysis and historical perspective.

In order to score highly you must be able to work accurately and quickly under pressure. The body of knowledge you need must be learnt in detail before you enter the examination. The key difference between a good student and a mediocre one lies in the ability to answer the question set, not the one you would like to answer in an ideal world. Examiners are restricted by what they can ask, because the focus of the examination derives solely from the key issues and content mentioned above. It is very important therefore that you ask your teacher to give you a copy of the specification so you can see exactly what you are being tested on. Examiners try to set papers that are challenging but fair. If you play by the rules, work hard and practise your essay-writing skills under timed conditions, you will be rewarded.

The biggest challenge facing you, as an AS student, is the difficulty of some of the concepts, ideas and language that confront you, especially after GCSE. The key is not to run away from these difficulties but to try to find a solution. You will no doubt be told by your teacher to read around the subject. This is crucial advice — good readers will show a significant improvement in the course of their studies. Read quality literature such as broadsheet newspapers and journals and make a note of phrases and ideas that you can include in your next essay. Your understanding of the course will improve dramatically as a result of this extra reading, and your written work, which is the key to doing well on this paper, will also improve.

How to use this guide

This guide has been designed to be as user-friendly as possible. It is not an exhaustive source, and you will need to supplement it with various other resources within the history department and from your school library. However, it is an essential revision tool, giving you a clear idea of the requirements of this option. There are three sections, as follows:

- **Introduction** — this section outlines the assessment objectives of the option, i.e. what you need to know in order to do well in the examination, as well as giving you ideas on how to revise and prepare thoroughly for the examination.
- **Content Guidance** — this section gives a review of the four study topics in the option, identified on p. 4. Some of the more difficult ideas and concepts you will need to master are outlined here. The ways in which this option can be linked to others within the specification are also shown.
- **Questions and Answers** — this section has a sample essay on each of the four study topics. Examiner comments point out what is missing from the answers and how the addition of new material would add to the marks in each case. These comments will help you to understand the skills and qualities that examiners are looking for in an A-grade answer and how a C-grade answer could be improved.

Revision planning

The OCR history specification is a modular course and there are a number of opportunities for you to take or retake individual modules. It is important that you learn to organise your time effectively. Learning how to revise and plan a programme in advance is obviously an important element for a successful student. Most students will be entered for this exam in the summer of the lower-sixth year, but some may wish to take advantage of January entry in that year. As every successful sportsperson is only too aware, the hard work is done months before the big race. This is exactly the same for examination preparation.

There are a number of general points about how to revise which apply to all subjects, such as trying to find a peaceful and quiet place to work, developing a routine and method which work for you, and revising in short, sharp sessions, when your mind is active and up to the task. Your ultimate aims when revising are twofold:

- to improve your knowledge and understanding of the course
- to understand how to tackle examination questions

Stage 1: planning

If you are being entered for the June module, you should begin to revise for your examination by the beginning of May at the latest. You will be given guidance from your teacher about what, when and how to revise. In most cases, revision will be based around the topics covered in class, but you will need to do a lot of work on your own in preparation for the timed tests you will have in this module. As you will be sitting examinations in other subjects, your time management and organisation need to be of the highest order, especially if you have commitments outside school. You need to be doing at least 5 hours of history revision a week in the final months of the academic year in preparation for the examination. Members of your history department will no doubt hold revision clinics and extra sessions to iron out any problems and fears you have before the examination.

Stage 2: making revision notes

It is important to remember that effective revision does not simply entail reading through your file. To be effective, revision needs to be active. You need to do something with the material in your files in order to learn and reinforce your understanding of the course. The first task is to write a good set of revision notes. These need to be clear, accurate, comprehensive (covering every element of your chosen study option) and easy to use.

Step 1: find the correct course notes in your book

It might be stating the obvious, but you need to know exactly what you are revising and where your notes are. You need to go over your class and homework notes on the four study topics, and ensure that all the factual gaps you may have left are filled. It would be a good idea to compare the Content Guidance section in this guide with the notes you have made throughout the year to ensure that everything is covered.

Step 2: read your notes carefully

You must spend a lot of time reading the notes you have made during the year. Do not skim read. If it helps, only read small chunks at a time. Make sure you understand what you are reading. If you do not understand something, check the relevant subject matter in the Content Guidance section of this guide. If something is still unclear, make a note of it and ask your teacher.

Step 3: highlight or underline key points

Once you have read a small chunk of notes, go back and read through it again. Then ask yourself: 'What were the most important points?' Use a highlighter or coloured pen to highlight these points.

Step 4: transfer key points to revision cards

Try to write down the key points you have highlighted without actually looking at your original notes. This will help you to check that you have understood what you have learnt and will build your confidence. Here are some tips to help you make good revision notes:

- Make notes on cards. These have the advantage of being smaller and less daunting than books or piles of paper. They are also stronger.
- Use coloured bullet points and underlining to help separate and clarify key points. Avoid long blocks of writing. You could use different colours for different aspects of your notes, e.g. red for titles/subtitles of main points; black for information; blue for examples, names, places etc.
- Use diagrams. These help you summarise material. It is often easier to remember a visual explanation than a written explanation.

Step 5: read your cards and put them away

Before going and doing something else, read the cards you have made once more to reinforce the information. You could get somebody to ask you questions about the topic you have been making notes on.

Stage 3: testing yourself

Revision does not end with making a set of notes. You must keep making sure that you remember the topics on which you have made notes. There are several ways to do this that can be done at different stages of your revision. Here are some ideas.

Brainstorming

This can be particularly helpful at the start of a revision session. If you have just made notes on Castlereagh's foreign policy, for example, you would need to check that you had remembered these before going on to look at Canning's foreign policy. Brainstorming simply involves writing down, or saying out loud, all the things you can remember about a topic. To start with, this should be done without any notes. When you have completely run out of ideas, look at your notes to see if there is anything you have forgotten. The result of a brainstorm should be a 'spider diagram' of ideas. Try to link these ideas before going on to something else.

Testing each other

Revising with a friend can be helpful at times. You could make up short one-word answer tests for each other. You could also explain events. Talking out loud forces you to clarify your ideas and demonstrates understanding.

Exam question tests

It is vital that your revision contains exam practice. You will do a lot of this in class and it is undoubtedly the most important element of revision.

- **Section A questions:** these are marked out of 30 and require you to **explain** or **examine** an event relevant to this option. Make sure that you use the Content

Guidance section in this guide to clarify your knowledge and have a look at the examples in the Question and Answer section to see student responses of different grades.

- **Section B questions:** these are generally more challenging as they are worth twice the marks. The key skills being tested here are **evaluation** and **analysis**, high-level skills acquired throughout the course. This is your opportunity to show exactly how well you understand the key issues you have been studying.

Examinable skills

It is worth asking yourself at the beginning of the course exactly what will be tested in the examination. If you can master the necessary skills, you are obviously going to be in a strong position to gain a high grade at the end of the course. In this module there are three assessment objectives (AOs) — these are the skills that are most important:

- AO1a requires you to recall, select and deploy historical knowledge accurately, and communicate knowledge and understanding of history in a clear and effective manner.
- AO1b asks you to present historical explanations, showing understanding of appropriate concepts, and to arrive at substantial judgements.
- AO2 is concerned with historical context, requiring you to interpret, evaluate and use a range of source material, and to explain and evaluate interpretations of the historical events and topics studied.

Essay writing

Essay writing must be in continuous prose using accurate grammar, punctuation and spelling. Be aware of use and style of language. Express yourself in unambiguous, uncluttered English.

The following points should be remembered:

- Short essays require you to be accurate and to write only relevant material — structure your answer around the question, exactly as it is asked. The point of the question must be kept in mind throughout the writing of the essay.
- When given an essay title, ask yourself, 'Do I understand it?' Identify the key words in the title and make sure you understand them. You should have an essay plan, but it needs to be flexible rather than static, so that you can adapt it to the precise terms of the question — its purpose should be to help you, not to impress the examiner. A small spider diagram might be useful.
- Ensure that in the examination you move away from rote-learned notes. Think afresh — do not trot out prepared essays. Originality is the key, so answer the question in front of you and not the one you would like to answer. You will be rewarded for factual recall, but you will receive far more credit for carefully and intelligently selected information to support a relevant argument.
- As a general rule (depending on the size of your writing), aim to fill at least four sides of paper for the two sub-questions. If you write much less it will be almost

impossible to cover all of the points you want to make in enough detail (although you will be required to write less in the first sub-question essay than the second). On the other hand, too much writing could mean you have said virtually everything on the topic and have lost the sharp focus that is vital for a high grade. Remember, the examination lasts for 1 hour and more time should be spent on sub-question B, where 60 marks are available.

- Challenge the assumption behind the question. Good history essays are argumentative and don't always agree with the title of the question. Some questions in Section B at AS have the phrases 'How far do you agree with...?' or 'Assess the view that...' Such questions are inviting you to give another viewpoint, not necessarily present in the title. In Section B, in particular, answers should pay due respect to the title, but also incorporate the importance of other factors in determining a historical judgement.
- Avoid using the expression 'I think' in your essay. It is bad style. Instead use, 'It can be said', 'One can say' or 'It can be argued'. Try also to avoid abbreviations such as 'Ind Rev' for 'Industrial Revolution'.

Essay structure

Imagine the writing of the essay to be like a courtroom drama unfolding before your eyes. The essay title is the criminal on trial. Every good essay should come in three distinct parts:

(1) Introduction
(2) The main body
(3) The conclusion

Introduction

Your task in the introduction is to give brief opening remarks for the defence and the prosecution (as any good lawyer would) using relevant supporting evidence. You should clearly understand what the question is asking and appreciate that there is an implicit paradox in it. For a Section B answer, aim to write around half a side. A good introduction will show that you have understood what the question is asking.

The main body

This is the core of the essay, where you give the detailed arguments for and against the question. Aim to write a minimum of two sides here. This should include a lot of evaluation and analysis and be supported with relevant, selective and precise evidence, where the factual material is fully focused on the question set. Paragraphs should be full and detailed, linking up with one another if appropriate. No stone should be left unturned until you have won the argument. You must also ensure that a balance has been struck between both elements of the question.

The conclusion

This is the climax of your essay, when you must reach a verdict, as a jury would have to do. Aim to write about half a side. Avoid the well-known pitfall of repeating what has already been said earlier or rewriting your introduction. The examiner knows

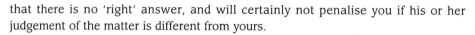

that there is no 'right' answer, and will certainly not penalise you if his or her judgement of the matter is different from yours.

Remember that examiners are aware of the enormous pressure you are under. They are mindful of what can be accomplished in 1 hour and are told to mark positively, not negatively. In addition, candidates will not be penalised for omitting facts that the examiner deems important, unless these are fundamental to the outcome of a judgement or evaluation.

Content
Guidance

There are four study topics in this option. They are:

(1) The age of Pitt and Liverpool, 1783–1830

(2) War and peace, 1793–1841

(3) The age of Peel, 1829–46

(4) The economy and industrialisation, 1780–1846

Each topic is divided into four key issues.

The aim of this section is to provide you with a skeleton version of what you need to learn for each study topic. This is followed by some more detailed information, introducing you to key ideas and personalities. This should give you the appropriate learning strategies needed to do well on this particular paper.

The examination paper will contain a choice of four questions, one on each study topic. You will have to answer one of these. Each question will be split into two sub-parts, dealing with any two of the key issues.

The age of Pitt and Liverpool, 1783–1830

The four key issues for study and examination are:

(1) Why did William Pitt the Younger dominate politics in the period 1783–93?
(2) How successfully did Pitt face the challenge of the French Revolution, 1789–1801?
(3) How and why was Lord Liverpool able to survive the radical challenges of 1812–22?
(4) How Liberal were the Tory governments of 1822–30?

Why did William Pitt the Younger dominate politics in the period 1783–93?

Summary

For this key issue you will need to know something of the background of William Pitt and his rapid rise to power by 1783. The reasons why he enjoyed the support of King George III will need to be studied and the reasons why Pitt was able to defeat the opposition Whig Party, led by Charles James Fox, in the famous election of 1784. You will also need to study Pitt's domestic policies as they relate to his reform of finance and administration and his development of overseas trade.

The question begins with the appointment of William Pitt the Younger as Prime Minister in 1783. Most will know that he was the youngest Prime Minister Britain has ever had. At just 24 years old he had already accumulated ministerial experience as Chancellor of the Exchequer in 1782 under a previous ministry and was well trained in the art of politics by his father, William Pitt the Elder, later the Earl of Chatham. Pitt was an extraordinary politician who possessed a remarkable ability for financial management and for administration. He was to need these qualities, as the position he inherited was far from secure. The disastrous American War of Independence had drained Britain's finances and had led to a humiliating loss of face for George III, the Hanoverian monarch. The opposition party — the Whigs — labelled the new regime 'The mince pie administration' because it was unlikely to survive beyond Christmas 1783.

Pitt, however, had several advantages, the most important of which was the support of the monarch, who decided when the next general election was to be called. As it turned out, Pitt was able to survive until March 1784, at which point he achieved a famous election victory. This triumph was the basis for the next 17 years of Pitt's first administration, and the Whigs lost a great deal of support and public sympathy. The King now had a stable ministry and, in the early years of his relationship with Pitt, a trusted confidante. Pitt was in a position to embark on an ambitious reforming programme up to 1793.

Financial policy

Defeat in the American War of Independence had created a major financial crisis for the Crown. The value of exports declined and the national debt — the amount of money the government owed — had risen dramatically to £242 million by 1784. Pitt therefore had to think of how to cut expenditure while raising taxes to meet the deficit. He was also keen to introduce a more efficient method of collecting these new taxes.

- **Imports and exports:** in 1784 Pitt introduced two measures aimed at curtailing the growing smuggling trade. A Commutation Act was designed to lower the import duty on tea and so make smuggling less profitable, and the introduction of a Hovering Act allowed smugglers' vessels to be searched up to 12 miles out to sea. Also, during the years 1785–87, duties on such items as brandy were reduced. This led to an increase in the value of food and raw material imports, exactly as Pitt wanted.
- **Taxation:** Pitt realised that the best way of raising new revenue would be through indirect taxes (purchase duties) on the rich. He therefore embarked on taxing the luxuries of the upper classes such as horses, wigs, hair powder and windows! He also hit the lower classes with taxes on candles. His taxation policy was generally successful and the amount reaching the Treasury improved dramatically — and almost doubled in some cases.
- **National debt:** in 1786 Pitt created the Sinking Fund. This was simply a means of reducing government debt by accumulating money. There was nothing original about such a venture, but as in all his financial dealings, Pitt ensured it was placed on a better footing. Commissioners were appointed to run it properly and to make sure it was not used to make up a shortfall in government revenue. In peacetime it worked well and by 1793, the national debt had been reduced by around £10 million. However, the outbreak of war with France in 1793 naturally raised the national debt and the Sinking Fund became less attractive. By 1820 Lord Liverpool had abandoned it.

Administrative policy

In his administrative policy, as elsewhere, Pitt aimed to cut out waste and improve efficiency in the running of government. He was also a great believer in one of the key ideas of the French Revolution — that positions in government should be open to talent and not inherited. Two important improvements in administration were made:

- **India:** in 1784 Pitt passed the India Act. This was designed primarily to remove the exclusive rights the East India Trading Company had in the financial administration of this ever-growing and financially lucrative area of the empire. A board of control was set up with Pitt himself as one of its members. It did not solve all the problems and the East India Company still retained a large say in India's administration; but it proved to be the foundation stone for successful administration when India became the 'jewel of the British empire' in the later nineteenth century.
- **Government waste:** cutting out government waste was another Pittite preoccupation and especially the excessive amount of patronage (granting positions of influence and money to a favourite) that the Crown exercised. However, he was

in a tricky situation, as George III was an immensely powerful political patron. In the event, government control over the Excise Board was strengthened and government financial accountability increased. Patronage was still in existence well into the nineteenth century, but Pitt's reforms in this area had sown seeds for future administrations to cultivate.

Trading policy

The development of trade was an equally important Pittite obsession. The disruption of trade as a result of the American War forced Pitt's government to widen Britain's trading horizons. Britain increased its trade with no fewer than eight European countries to make up the shortfall left by the loss of the USA. The idea of free trade was a concept Pitt had embraced after reading Adam Smith's treatise *The Wealth of Nations*, and he passionately believed that having trade barriers between countries was more politically than economically dangerous. He promised to do all in his power to improve laissez-faire economics in Europe. (Laissez-faire means to leave alone — and thus to reduce government interference in the economy.)

The most famous trade treaty signed by Pitt's government was the **Eden Treaty** with France, signed in 1786. This was an important agreement which gave citizens of Britain and France free access to each other's countries, as well as reducing the number of tariffs (taxes on imported goods) on selected items. British manufacturers were especially grateful to the government in finding new areas for their products and tended to do better than their French counterparts. The outbreak of war in 1793, however, proved the treaty's undoing, and it was abandoned soon after.

Conclusion

Pitt the Younger was able to dominate politics between 1783 and 1793 primarily because of:

- **the continued support of King George III**, still arguably Britain's most powerful politician
- **the division of his Whig opponents**, especially after their reaction to the French Revolution (see below)
- **the dominance Pitt exercised in the conduct of domestic policy**, especially in the areas outlined above

How successfully did Pitt face the challenge of the French Revolution, 1789–1801?

Summary

The outbreak of revolution in France during the summer of 1789 and its consequences in England during the 1790s form the basis of this key issue. The way in which Pitt dealt with the radical threat should be studied as well as the way in which the French Revolution split his main rivals for power, the Whigs. This party had a number of leading personalities such as Edmund Burke, Charles James Fox and the Duke of Portland, all of whom disagreed on the future of their party as a result of the revolution in France. You should also study how William Pitt was able to use these differences to split the opposition and win some of them over to his Tory Party by 1794.

Reactions to the revolution

The start of the French Revolution was arguably the most important event in modern history and cast a shadow over European politics. The overthrow of the French aristocracy and the rallying cry of 'Liberty, Equality and Fraternity' had a devastating impact on the ruling classes in France. The revolution was initially welcomed in England, especially by the Whig opposition leader Charles James Fox, who claimed 'the greatest event...that ever happened in the world' had broken out. This enthusiasm saw the establishment of a number of organisations committed to their own 'English Revolution', such as the Sheffield Society for Constitutional Information and the more influential London Corresponding Society (LCS). The radicals' main inspiration was two volumes by **Thomas Paine** entitled *The Rights of Man*. In these volumes, Paine passionately supported the right of the people to overthrow aristocratic government and even talked about the establishment of a republic.

The revolution could not have come at a worse time for Pitt. Between 1788 and 1789 his position was undermined by the first outbreak of George III's mental illness that modern scientists have identified as porphyria. The prospect of the King stepping aside for the pro-Whig Prince of Wales was a real concern for the Prime Minister. In the event, he was rescued both by the recovery of the King and by Whig divisions over how to approach the revolution. Fox was extremely enthusiastic. Yet fellow Whigs such as Edmund Burke did not share his enthusiasm. Burke's *Reflections on the Revolution in France* (published in 1791), in which he condemned the bloodshed and anarchy occurring in France, proved to be the bible of loyalism. The split between Burke and Fox was widened by Burke's *Appeal From the New to the Old Whigs*, in which he condemned Fox for supporting the revolution.

In addition, two of Fox's closest political allies, Grey and Whitbread, were demanding parliamentary reform as events in France were becoming more extreme, a fact which alienated Whig landowners even further. Pitt saw an opportunity to win over aristocratic Whigs who disapproved of Fox's radicalism and create the first broad-based aristocratic Conservative administration. This finally occurred in 1794, when leading Whigs such as the Duke of Portland deserted Fox. His opposition became even more ineffective between 1794 and 1801.

Pitt's anti-radical legislation

Pitt was determined to stamp out the radical threat, which seemed to be strongest in the cities and which was dominated in membership by skilled artisans and craftsmen.

In the light of the effect Thomas Paine was having on an increasingly literate working class, two royal proclamations were passed in 1792 against what were labelled 'seditious writings'. Using spies and *agents provocateurs*, Pitt exaggerated the nature of the radical threat and established a Committee of Secrecy to monitor their activity. During the period 1792–1801, a number of laws were passed aimed at blunting the radical message:

- **Suspension of the Habeas Corpus Amendment Act:** from May 1794 to July 1795 and again in 1798–1801, anyone could be arrested and held indefinitely merely on suspicion of having committed a crime.
- **The Seditious Meetings Act** and **Treasonable Practices Act, 1795:** known as the 'Two Acts', these banned meetings that hadn't been approved by the local magistrate and broadened the definition of treason to allow more arrests. They were precipitated by the stoning of the King's coach by an unruly London mob and the return of a difficult economic situation, mainly as a result of the war.
- **The Act Against Unlawful Oaths, 1797:** this law, which increased the penalty for undermining authority, was passed following a mutiny in the Navy.
- **Defence of the Realm Act, 1798:** this required information to be given and volunteer militias to be set up, ready to fight for King and country. This was especially important as an abortive French invasion was attempted at Fishguard, west Wales, in the same year.
- **Combination Laws, 1799:** this ban on the 'combination' of men effectively abolished trade unions. It especially hit the radical movement, as the trade union was the only method working men had of redressing grievances against an unscrupulous employer.

The opposition claimed that England was living under a repressive regime that rode roughshod over individual liberties. Strangely, people welcomed this harsh legislation to root out dangerous 'Jacobins' — supporters of the French Revolution in England. The 1790s witnessed the creation of many loyalist associations, such as that founded in 1792 by John Reeves 'for the Preservation of Property against Republicans and Levellers', in support of the King and country. They attacked radical meetings knowing that the local magistrates would turn a blind eye to their activities. Pitt was successfully winning a propaganda war in which Jacobinism meant disloyalty to the sacred institution of monarchy under the much-loved George III. He was helped by the French execution of their king, Louis XVI, in 1792 and the patriotism aroused by the declaration of war between France and England a year later.

Conclusion

Pitt successfully met the challenge of the French Revolution between 1789 and 1801 by:

- exploiting **Whig divisions** in their response to the French Revolution
- introducing strong and successful **anti-Jacobin legislation**
- ensuring that he won the **propaganda war**, especially after the execution of the French king in 1792 and the declaration of war in 1793

- having **loyalist support** from the majority of the people, especially towards King George III

The strong political alliance that existed between Pitt and George III was ended over Irish affairs at the turn of the century. **The Act of Union** signed between Ireland and England in 1800 was an important turning point. Pitt wanted Catholics to be allowed to become MPs (**Roman Catholic emancipation**) and take up their seats in the Parliament in London. George III refused to agree to this, leaving Pitt and his followers no option but to leave office. Pitt returned as Prime Minister in 1805, but his ministry was cut short by ill health. He died in 1806.

How and why was Lord Liverpool able to survive the radical challenges of 1812–22?

Summary

Lord Liverpool was Prime Minister of Britain, 1812–27, but was faced with many difficulties, especially up to 1822. The way he dealt with these problems, by introducing unpopular laws such as the Corn Law of 1815 and the severe policies he introduced against the radical opposition, forms the focus of this key issue. You also need to understand why he was able to survive some pretty unpopular times and continue as Prime Minister.

The Tory Party in power, 1812–30

Following the assassination of Spencer Perceval in 1812, Lord Liverpool was appointed Prime Minister. He was an experienced politician and an enthusiastic Pittite, who faced a difficult task from when he took office until his stroke in 1827. He led the Tory Party and was determined to rule the country with the support of the aristocracy and landowners, who dominated the political scene in England at this time. The working classes and radicals were not as enthusiastic and saw the opportunity to present their grievances.

The problems facing the country at this time were numerous:
- **National debt:** the cost of the war was mounting — the national debt had increased to £902 million by 1816. This of course had to be paid for, and the working classes had to pay more through an increase in indirect taxes — on beer, for example. Yet the rich were far from exempt because in 1799 Pitt had introduced an income tax on property owners to help pay for the war.
- **Urban poverty:** industrialisation brought squalor to the working classes in the cities as they lived in terrible housing, had a poor diet and the government failed to alleviate their distress with the provision of education or welfare services.

- **Rural poverty:** there were problems in the countryside, as the enclosure movement forced some poorer farmers off the land, and farmers suffered when prices dropped when the war was over in 1815.
- **Voting rights:** the lower classes were unable to make themselves heard because they did not have the vote. Voting rights could only be claimed at this point if you possessed enough property, giving the landowning aristocracy a great deal of power.
- **Unemployment:** the end of the war brought its own problems. The reduction in demand for goods associated with the war and the demobilisation of some 400,000 soldiers swelled the ranks of the unemployed.

Some historians, such as Professor Norman Gash, have claimed it took 50 years to bring these problems under control. Lord Liverpool was therefore faced with huge difficulties when the country should have been celebrating a great victory over Napoleon Bonaparte.

The challenge of the radical movement, 1812–22

The radical movement was able to make great headway in such a difficult situation. They demanded a fairer political system in which the masses (such as factory workers, artisans, croppers, weavers and the unemployed) had a say. Between 1812 and 1822 they expressed their protests in a variety of ways:

- **Luddites** showed their hatred of industrialisation by smashing machinery, especially in areas such as the East Midlands and Yorkshire between 1811 and 1816.
- There were a number of protests such as the **Spa Field Riots** in 1816, the **March of the Blanketeers** and the **Pentrich Rising** in 1817.
- The most serious protests occurred in Manchester in 1819 when a large crowd that had assembled at **St Peter's Fields** was turned on by the local authorities, resulting in the death of 11 protesters.
- **The Cato Street Conspiracy** of 1820 was an attempt by a leading group of radicals, known as the Spenceans, to blow up the whole Cabinet. Although the plan failed, it showed how serious the radical movement was in its hatred of Lord Liverpool's government.
- The climax of radical success occurred during the so-called **Queen Caroline Affair**, which lasted from 1820 to 1821. The attempt by Queen Caroline to discredit the Tory government and the hated King George IV was used by the radicals as an excuse to riot in support of the estranged Queen, when she returned to England to claim her rights. Lord Liverpool's government almost fell and the whole episode led to the resignation of two Cabinet members.

Liverpool's response to these radical threats was to pursue firm government on behalf of the aristocracy. In 1815 he passed the famous **Corn Law**. As mentioned above, English agriculture had been experiencing a difficult time, following a series of poor harvests. The situation for farmers grew worse as the country was flooded by cheap imports of grain. Bread was the staple diet of the lower classes and government policy had a direct bearing on their livelihood — and in some cases their survival. Liverpool decided that the English landowners should be protected from cheap grain to ensure their profits remained stable. Put simply, English grain had to be at a competitive price before foreign grain was allowed into the country. This measure won great support from farmers and landowners, but meant that the price of bread would always remain high for the consumer now that cheaper foreign grain was not allowed into the country.

Liverpool also outraged the working classes when he abolished income tax in 1816, thus easing the tax burden on the rich. He raised indirect taxes further (taxes on goods), which affected the poorer classes greatly, and in the same year passed the Game Laws, making poaching punishable by imprisonment or transportation to Australia.

Liverpool's anti-radical legislation

In his defence, it should be said that Lord Liverpool had no real precedent to fall back on in tackling the radical opposition, save perhaps the situation faced by Pitt in the 1790s. Liverpool decided (as Pitt had done) that the only way to survive was by using repressive legislation. There was no national police force at that time, and the radicals were thought (incorrectly as it turned out) to be well armed, so Liverpool felt that he had no alternative until the situation improved. He had also seen the example of the French Revolution, which had developed into anarchy when the lower classes were allowed to set the political agenda. He therefore introduced the following measures:

- **Suspension of the Habeas Corpus Amendment Act, 1817:** following the Spa Fields Riots in December 1816, Liverpool decided to suspend habeas corpus, as Pitt had done. This meant that the government could hold someone suspected of radical activity for an indefinite period. It was intended as a temporary measure, lasting only until 1818.
- **Seditious Meetings Act, 1817:** again reacting to a radical threat, Liverpool followed Pitt's precedent with another Seditious Meetings Act. This forbade the unlawful assembly of more than 50 people and imposed the death penalty for mutiny in the armed forces.
- **Six Acts, 1819:** arguably the most repressive piece of anti-radical legislation in this period, these were passed as a response to the St Peter's Fields protest in Manchester (see above) and were intended to prevent any attack on the state. The legislation gave magistrates the power to restrict the activities of the radical press as well as facilitating ways in which opponents of the regime could be convicted in a court of law. Modern historians, however, do not believe that the sinister reputation of the Six Acts is borne out by the facts; they were again intended as a temporary measure until the storm clouds had passed.

Conclusion

Liverpool was able to survive the radical challenge for the following reasons:

- **Weakness of postwar radicalism:** the cause was divided, lacked weaponry and was only strong in industrialised areas. It never really had control of the capital city.

- **Legislation to meet the radical threat:** the suspension of habeas corpus and the Six Acts worked, despite their unpopularity.
- **Use of espionage:** spies were used to infiltrate the opposition.
- **Support of local yeomanry and army:** they were used to intimidate opponents, but in some cases (such as Peterloo) their reaction led to further violence.
- **Determination:** Liverpool kept his nerve throughout the period. He also realised that he would bring in more popular policies once the worst of the crisis was over.

How Liberal were the Tory governments of 1822–30?

Summary

The final key issue for this study topic focuses on whether the Tory governments changed their attitude and became less severe and more 'Liberal'. Ministers such as William Huskisson introduced a series of important reforms that might suggest they did become more Liberal. However, there are also examples we can use from this period to claim that the Tory governments were anti-Liberal, by virtue of the fact that they ignored calls for Catholic emancipation and demands for parliamentary reform.

Liverpool and Liberalism

Allegedly, Liverpool embarked upon a more Liberal (less repressive) period from 1822. This has caused much controversy among historians, with some questioning whether the change took place.

On the face of it, there did seem to be a more Liberal direction in government policy following the end of the Queen Caroline Affair in 1820–21:
- A generation of newer and **younger politicians** came into the Cabinet. For example, William Huskisson was appointed President of the Board of Trade, Frederick Robinson was made Chancellor of the Exchequer, Sir Robert Peel was appointed Home Secretary and George Canning followed Castlereagh as Foreign Secretary.
- William Huskisson was determined to improve Britain's trading position with the rest of the world, based on the philosophy of **free trade**, by repealing the Navigation Laws. His most famous reform was the passing of the Reciprocity of Duties Act in 1823. This allowed foreign ships to enter British ports on the same basis as their British counterparts. This he hoped would be seen as a good-will gesture towards Britain's competitors and reduce the costs to British manufacturers. Huskisson also relaxed trade restrictions with British colonies. The colonies could now trade with foreign countries for the first time, but the mother country hoped to retain the majority of business by providing subsidies to the colonies.

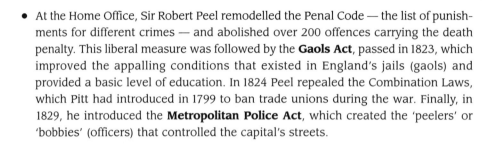

- At the Home Office, Sir Robert Peel remodelled the Penal Code — the list of punishments for different crimes — and abolished over 200 offences carrying the death penalty. This liberal measure was followed by the **Gaols Act**, passed in 1823, which improved the appalling conditions that existed in England's jails (gaols) and provided a basic level of education. In 1824 Peel repealed the Combination Laws, which Pitt had introduced in 1799 to ban trade unions during the war. Finally, in 1829, he introduced the **Metropolitan Police Act**, which created the 'peelers' or 'bobbies' (officers) that controlled the capital's streets.

An alternative view

There were, however, a number of issues that split the Tory Party, especially after the death of Lord Liverpool in 1828. These call into question the appropriateness of the term 'Liberal Tory', as applied to the Tory governments between 1822 and 1830. Some historians have argued that continuity, not change, between this period and the former one can be seen, and that the distinction between a reactionary and a Liberal phase in Liverpool's administration is misleading. There are a number of issues that call into question the term 'Liberal' in the period 1822–30:

- Although Wellington was made Prime Minister in 1828, he embarked on a number of disastrous policies for the Tory Party. In 1828, for example, he **repealed the Test and Corporation Acts**. These Acts, passed in the seventeenth century, prevented dissenters or nonconformists (non-members of the Church of England) from holding municipal office. As most dissenters were supporters of the Whigs, repeal of the Acts gave them an extra base of support. It also threatened the basis of Anglican control — the official Church of England, a strong supporter of the Tory Party. The laws were not repealed, though, because the Tory government had suddenly turned 'Liberal'. Repeal of the Acts was a compromise acceptable to the Tory administration at the time. It did not eliminate all discrimination against dissenters since they were still excluded from Oxford and Cambridge universities and could still be married only by an Anglican minister.

- Catholics felt that, if nonconformists had punitive restrictions removed in 1828, there was no reason why they should not be given similar treatment. Catholics in Ireland were especially upset that, since the Act of Union in 1800, they were unable to sit as MPs in the British Parliament. Ultra Tories viewed with horror the prospect of granting any concessions to the untrustworthy Catholics (who also held strong allegiance to the Pope) and Peel, as Home Secretary, was known to be one of the Ultras' strongest supporters. In 1829, however, Peel was **forced to grant Roman Catholic emancipation** to avoid civil war in Ireland, when Daniel O'Connell challenged the laws that forbade Catholics to become MPs. The Ultras were incensed at Wellington and Peel, whom they accused of betraying the party. The party had been forced to give in to O'Connell and could hardly be claimed to be Liberal in this instance.

- Throughout the period 1822–30, Tory governments had consistently **refused to entertain the idea of parliamentary reform**. They believed that landowners were the best people to run the country and refused to give the vote to either the middle or the lower classes. This, again, cannot be regarded as promoting Liberal Tory government.

Conclusion

The question of how Liberal the Tory governments were in this period therefore remains open. In support of the view, you could point to:

- the appointment of **younger politicians** as a result of the Cabinet reshuffle of 1822–23
- the **Liberal economic legislation** of Huskisson and Robinson
- the **reforms of Peel** at the Home Office

You could, however, note the following points to show that the Tory governments were not Liberal:

- their initial **refusal to accept Roman Catholic emancipation** in 1829
- the **repeal of the Test and Corporation Acts** in 1828
  (Both changes were ultimately forced upon them.)
- their absolute **refusal to reform Parliament and give more people the vote**

War and peace, 1793–1841

The four key issues for study and examination are:

(1) What were British foreign policy interests in the period 1793–1841?
(2) How and why did Britain win such a long war with France, 1793–1815?
(3) How successful was Castlereagh in securing an effective peace at Vienna, and from 1814 to 1822?
(4) How effectively did Canning and Palmerston secure British interests, 1822–41?

What were British foreign policy interests in the period 1793–1841?

Summary

Britain's foreign policy interests in this period included the need for strategic security, both in Europe and in a world context. The maintenance of British trading interest was an obvious priority, given Britain's growing empire, as was the power of its navy, in the defence of its islands. Finally, all British foreign secretaries were concerned to maintain the balance of power — making sure that no one country was powerful enough to threaten the interests of the other Great Powers (Austria, France, Russia and Prussia).

Strategic security

Strategic security for Britain and its colonies was of vital importance. The reason Britain declared war with France in 1793 was to preserve its relationship with the Dutch. After 1815 the biggest threat to strategic security was assumed to be Russia. This was primarily because the Russians had their eye on the territories of the Turkish empire, which was assumed to be on the point of collapse. Relations with the USA were also dictated by strategic security for Canada, which seemed to be particularly vulnerable after the loss of the USA in 1783.

Trade

Trade was especially important for Britain at this time. The expansion of the empire, especially after the Treaty of Vienna in 1815, saw the establishment of trading posts throughout the world — for example, the Cape of Good Hope in South Africa. A larger empire created new and exciting opportunities for business, which successive governments vowed to protect. In 1839, for example, Britain and China found themselves at war over access to the lucrative opium trade.

Naval power

Britain had always placed a great deal of emphasis on having a strong navy, due mainly to the desire to protect its island status. Britain's navy was stronger than that of any of its competitors in this period, and it was used not only for protection but also as a vital aggressive tool in war. Nelson's great naval victory in 1805 at Trafalgar was one of the most decisive battles of the Napoleonic Wars. Later, Palmerston developed the idea of 'gunboat diplomacy' as a warning to Britain's rivals if they threatened its interests. Naval power was also used to police the empire and search vessels engaged in the Atlantic slave trade.

Balance of power

This concept dominated the whole of nineteenth-century British foreign policy. It was the idea that all the Great Powers should act together to create a balance of power that would prevent any one country becoming too powerful. The massive growth of the French empire under Napoleon had provided the precedent, but the greatest potential threat after 1815 was Russia and its designs on the Near East.

Conclusion

In foreign policy, British interests in this period tended to overlap but can be summarised as:

- ensuring that the **strategic security of the empire** remained intact (especially after the loss of America in 1783)
- **expanding overseas trade** by acquiring trading posts and new opportunities for business
- **using the navy** to ensure that its interests were being protected across the globe

- **maintaining the balance of power** in Europe and around the world, especially in North and South America

How and why did Britain win such a long war with France, 1793–1815?

Summary

Britain and France were almost continuously at war with one another between 1793 and 1815. For this key issue you need to understand why Britain and its allies emerged victorious. There are a number of reasons, such as the power of the British navy as shown by the defeat of the French at Trafalgar in 1805. You also need to understand how a coalition determined to defeat Napoleon Bonaparte was maintained, and how important it was for Britain to fund its allies, especially at the start of the war. Finally, you need to study the importance of the military campaign in Spain and the emergence of Arthur Wellesley, later the Duke of Wellington.

Naval strategy

William Pitt was certainly not expecting a war to break out in 1793, but French designs on Holland threatened Britain's trading interests and threatened to upset the balance of power in northern Europe. When war was finally declared on 1 February 1793, Pitt believed it would be a short affair, restricted to that area. He was wrong, however, with the war lasting almost continuously until Napoleon's final defeat in the summer of 1815. Throughout the war, Pitt and subsequent leaders placed a great deal of emphasis on the power of the navy. Napoleon was known to be a brilliant army commander, but his mastery of the sea was less secure. The capture of various French possessions in the West Indies between 1794 and 1796, using naval power, was vital both strategically and economically. Massive sums were spent re-equipping the navy and by 1801, 133,000 men served in it. Britain was also fortunate to possess some celebrated admirals such as Keith, Jervis and Collingwood, but arguably the greatest was Nelson. He was a constant thorn in the French side, as his victories at Aboukir Bay in 1798, against the Danish at Copenhagen in 1801, and ultimately at Trafalgar in 1805 prove. Nonetheless, everyone knew that the navy was a defensive weapon that could not win the war on its own. There were other important factors behind France's defeat.

Coalition diplomacy, finance and subsidies

The war against France was a collective effort; even before Britain entered it, Austria and Prussia had declared war, fearful of the spread of revolutionary ideals into their territories. Russia would join at a later stage to provide much needed back-up in the East. They were all kept together by the common aim of defeating Napoleon, and pledged themselves to one another in a number of alliances or coalitions.

This collective team spirit was vitally important in defeating Napoleon, especially between 1812 and 1815, when the expert diplomatic skills of Castlereagh were needed. Yet it wasn't always a natural cooperation, as at various stages of the war Napoleon managed to divide and rule the allies. Britain had to buy their loyalty. Total subsidies to Britain's allies throughout the war amounted to £66m, much to the resentment of the taxpayer. Pitt, however, was meaner and refused to commit more than a miserly £9.2m, up to the brief Peace of Amiens in 1802.

Military strategy on the peninsula

The most crucial phase of the war began in 1808 on the Iberian peninsula. Napoleon called this campaign 'the Spanish ulcer' as it was to plague him on numerous occasions up to 1813. Britain initially became involved in order to support Portugal against increased French influence and to support Spanish rebels, who were determined to overthrow their king — Napoleon's hated brother Joseph. The campaign was a military triumph for Arthur Wellesley, created Viscount Wellington in 1809 and Duke in 1812, forcing Napoleon to split his forces at a time when he was planning the crucial invasion of Russia in 1812. In addition, Wellington was able to invade France via the Pyrenees as well as having a continental base from which to check Napoleon's ambitions. Famous victories over the French at Vimiero, Talavera, Salamanca and Vitoria, as well as the defence of Lisbon along the lines of the Torres Vedras, were hailed as military triumphs and were one of the major turning points in the war. Despite the fact that the British army numbered no more than 60,000, it had the advantages of Wellington's expert military leadership as well as support from the local population.

Conclusion

Britain was therefore able to win the long war against France due to:
- its **naval power**
- the **economic strength** it enjoyed as a result of the Industrial Revolution
- the **subsidies and finance** it provided to its allies
- the **coalition diplomacy** that kept the alliance together
- the turning point provided by **Wellington's success** on the Iberian peninsula
- **Napoleon's growing ambitions**, especially his invasion of Russia in 1812
- **Napoleon's mental and physical exhaustion**, especially after the loss of Spain

How successful was Castlereagh in securing an effective peace at Vienna, and from 1814 to 1822?

Summary

The peace negotiations that ended the Napoleonic Wars took place at Vienna in 1815. Britain's representative was Viscount Castlereagh, Foreign Secretary until 1822.

The focus of this key issue is on how successful Castlereagh was in representing Britain's interests through the creation of the Quadruple Alliance and the development of the Congress system. Also of relevance is his role in the collapse of the Congress system; for example, the State Paper of 1820 in which he regretfully turned his back on his European allies.

Negotiations at Vienna, 1815

The peacemakers met at Vienna in 1815 to try to redraw the map of Europe after the upheaval of the previous 23 years. Britain's representative was Viscount Castlereagh, Foreign Secretary from 1812 to 1822. He made his attitude fairly clear from an early stage when he said, 'It is not our business to collect trophies, but to try, if we can, to bring the world back to peaceful habits'. He and the other peacemakers from Austria, Russia and Prussia shared the same principles, namely to:

- create a European balance of power
- contain France by strengthening the countries that shared its borders
- restore legitimate monarchs to their thrones
- reward the victors
- punish France

Britain did not receive any mainland European territory but instead was given trading outposts: Malta in the Mediterranean, Tobago and St Lucia in the Caribbean and the important Cape of Good Hope from the Dutch. Singapore would soon follow and Britain's control of India was assured. Castlereagh was very successful in maintaining Britain's interests at Vienna, and its prestige as both a European and world power had never been greater.

The Congress system

As noted above, Castlereagh's diplomacy towards the end of the Napoleonic Wars was one of the major reasons for British success. Apart from concluding a lasting peace treaty, he wished to continue this wartime cooperation into a peacetime situation, and at the Second Treaty of Paris in 1815 he was the leading light in the formation of the **Quadruple Alliance** between Britain, Austria, Russia and Prussia. Apart from general cooperation, they all agreed to meet from time to time to discuss the affairs of Europe. This treaty and the other agreements made in the closing stages of the war laid the foundation for the so-called 'Congress system', which was to last until around 1830.

Initially, the Great Powers agreed with one another, and at the first Congress, at Aix-la-Chapelle (Aachen) in 1818, France was added to the Quadruple Alliance. Yet beneath the surface there were growing splits between Britain and France on the one hand and the eastern powers (Austria, Russia and Prussia) on the other. The major disagreement was whether the troops of the Congress system could be used to crush internal revolutions that affected legitimate authority. At the Congress of Troppau in 1820, held against the background of revolution in Spain and Naples, the eastern powers agreed they could be. Castlereagh refused to sign, and justified his rejection to a packed

House of Commons in his famous **State Paper** of May 1820. From this point on, Britain was only an observer in European affairs at the remaining two Congresses held at Laibach in 1821 and Verona in 1822.

Conclusion

Castlereagh was a highly successful Foreign Secretary who during this period managed to uphold British interests as well as being one of the leading lights in the creation of a settlement at Vienna, which lasted well beyond his lifetime. His vision of a Congress system was an inspired idea, but failed largely because of the selfish interests of some other members. By 1820 Britain's involvement had come to an end, much to the sadness of its founder. Castlereagh's suicide in 1822 led to the appointment of George Canning as Foreign Secretary.

How effectively did Canning and Palmerston secure British interests, 1822–41?

Summary

The study of two famous British foreign secretaries, George Canning (1822–27) and Viscount Palmerston (1830–41), forms the core of this key issue. Their policies as regards the 'Eastern Question' — Britain's desire to keep the Turkish empire together — is particularly important, as are British foreign relations with Belgium, France, Spain and the USA during their periods of office. Both men had a keen interest in ensuring the abolition of slavery and Palmerston had dealings with China over the opium trade.

The Greek Revolt

The first problem to confront Canning was the Eastern Question. The maintenance of the Turkish empire was of great importance to Britain because Russia, in particular, was keen to obtain territory in the area at Turkey's expense. The outbreak of the Greek Revolt in 1821 against Turkish rule created a dilemma for Canning, as public opinion in England sided with the Greeks. Of greater concern was Russian support for the Greek demands for independence. Canning was afraid that Russia would intervene and create a permanent presence in the area. Matters were not helped when Mehemet Ali, ruler of Egypt, and an ally of Turkey, successfully crushed the revolt. Through a combination of diplomacy and force, the situation was resolved and Greece finally gained its independence in 1830 with the Treaty of London.

Relations with the Congress powers

The outbreak of the Spanish Revolution in 1820 worsened relations between Britain and its Congress partners. The eastern powers (Austria, Russia and Prussia) and

France wanted to use the Troppau Protocol to restore legitimate rule to Spain. (The Troppau Protocol was signed by Austria, Prussia and Russia and stated that it was justifiable for force to be used to restore rulers to their thrones if they had been overthrown by revolution.) Canning reluctantly agreed in April 1823 but managed to negotiate the **Polignac Memorandum**, in which France agreed not to intervene in Spain's colonies in South America. In 1824 Canning recognised the independence of Spain's former colonies and showed that Britain was capable of taking independent action, ensuring that Britain's global trading interests remained intact. Canning also successfully thwarted Spanish designs on Portugal in 1826 and won a major diplomatic victory. Canning believed that the Congress system was limiting national independence and that Britain was being dictated to by Austria, Prussia and Russia. He took much satisfaction in its demise during this period. When Liverpool had his fateful stroke in 1827, Canning was appointed Prime Minister, but died in office the same year.

The Belgian Revolt

In 1830 the Whig Party triumphed in a general election and the Tories, who had been in office since 1812, were cast into the wilderness. There were, however, many similarities between the foreign policies of the two parties.

John Henry Temple, third Viscount Palmerston, became Foreign Secretary in Earl Grey's Whig administration. When he came to office the Belgian Revolt had broken out. The Belgians wanted independence from their Dutch masters and initially Palmerston viewed their demands for independence positively. Yet he was equally concerned about French interference in what they regarded as a legitimate sphere of influence. The eastern powers supported the Dutch demands that legitimacy should be restored. Palmerston was in a very difficult situation. He wanted to support Belgium, but not at the expense of French involvement; neither did he want the situation to turn into a major European war with the involvement of the other powers. Luck played into his hands when a revolt broke out in Poland in 1830, distracting the three eastern powers. The whole episode dragged on until 1839, when the Dutch finally recognised Belgian independence. Palmerston came out of the episode with great credit by thwarting French aims in the area and ensuring that a strategic balance was maintained.

Policy towards Spain and Portugal

Palmerston, in the same way as Canning, was determined to preserve the independence of Portugal and Spain from increased French influence. A series of crises in the 1830s produced a situation where pro-British interests were threatened by Spanish and French claims to their respective crowns. Palmerston's response to these threats was the creation of a new **Quadruple Alliance** (1834) signed by Britain, France, Portugal and Spain. This agreement, Palmerston hoped, would restrain Spanish and French influence on the Iberian peninsula and preserve British interests.

Once again, Palmerston had emerged from a potentially difficult situation with great credit.

Near Eastern crises, 1831–41

Palmerston was faced with two crises in the Near East between 1831 and 1841. The first broke out when he was distracted by the Reform Bill crisis at home and was more of a bystander as events unfolded. Mehemet Ali, the Egyptian leader, attacked Turkish interests and defeated the Turks at **Konieh** in 1832. The Turks appealed to the Russians for help and a formal treaty was signed at **Unkiar Skelessi** in 1833. This gave Syria (part of the Turkish empire) to Mehemet Ali and, in a secret clause, allowed the Russian navy to enter the Mediterranean through the Bosphorus and Dardanelles Straits. Palmerston was worried about Russian and French involvement in the area, and its possible impact on British trade, and from 1833 onwards developed a more consistent policy towards Turkey that culminated in an Anglo–Turkish Trade Convention, signed in 1838. Palmerston had managed to salvage something for Britain, but was determined to be better prepared when the next flashpoint occurred.

Turkey was determined to regain Syria but was defeated by a joint Egyptian–French force in 1839. Palmerston was now faced with the increased prospect of French involvement in the Turkish empire as well as the threat of Russia intervening to help Turkey. He could not afford to be left behind on this occasion and resolved that the best solution lay with **multilateral diplomacy** (ensuring all parties are involved in negotiations). Palmerston first arranged the **Convention of London (1840)**, which was signed by Britain, Austria, Russia and Prussia. France was furious at being excluded and a realistic possibility of war between Britain and France loomed. By the terms of the Convention, Egyptian forces were to be withdrawn from Syria. Ali refused to agree but changed his mind when British gunboats bombed Alexandria and Acre was captured in 1840. The following year, in July 1841, the **Straits Convention** was signed. This forbade the passage of warships through the Bosphorus and Dardanelles, thus cancelling the privileges of the Unkiar Skelessi treaty. Palmerston emerged from the whole episode with huge credit. He had managed to avoid war, but preserve the independence of Turkey while discrediting France through diplomacy.

Relations with the USA

Relations with the USA in this period were dominated by the slave trade. Palmerston was determined that the Americans would abide by an agreement signed between the two countries in 1807, in which the USA had agreed to outlaw the slave trade. The only way Britain could be sure the agreement was being adhered to would be to introduce a '**right of search**', allowing Britain to board, and in extreme cases confiscate, American ships suspected of carrying slaves. Not surprisingly, the US government was unhappy with the situation and relations between the two countries remained very tense.

The Opium War with China

Palmerston was also determined to uphold British trading interests in China. The main issue concerned the opium trade, which was lucrative for Britain. Opium was in widespread use in Europe, but the Chinese did not want to legalise the trade in it and the issue sparked a war when China seized opium belonging to the East India Company in 1839. Britain's naval power ensured that the war was over swiftly and in the **Treaty of Nanking (1842)** Britain was given Hong Kong, as well as six other ports on the Chinese mainland, and £6m in compensation from the Chinese government.

Conclusion

Both Canning and Palmerston were quite effective in securing British interests between 1822 and 1841. In the Near East the threat of Mehemet Ali had been repelled, while in Europe both foreign secretaries had restrained France and Spain from intervening when Britain's interests were threatened. Relations with the USA were tolerable, but a lot of negotiation would still be needed, especially over the slave trade. Canning had ensured that the outcome of the Greek Revolt did not sacrifice British interests, while Palmerston had secured abundant trading opportunities in China. Above all, both men realised that it was essential to preserve the independence of the Turkish empire and restrict Russian influence.

The age of Peel, 1829–46

The four key issues for study and examination are:
(1) Why was Ireland so important for Peel's career?
(2) How effective was Peel as a party political leader?
(3) Why is Peel's ministry of 1841–46 considered to be so successful?
(4) Why did Corn Law repeal lead to the collapse of Peel's government in 1846?

Why was Ireland so important for Peel's career?

Summary

Sir Robert Peel's relations with Ireland form a crucial element of his career. This key issue requires you to study his career as it was affected by Irish concerns, starting with the passage of Roman Catholic emancipation in 1829, when he allowed Catholics to sit as MPs at Westminster. His relations with Daniel O'Connell will also need to be studied, as will the various Irish policies he introduced as Prime Minister between 1841 and 1846, such as the passage of the controversial Maynooth Grant in 1845, which

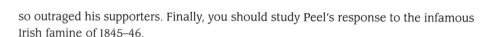

so outraged his supporters. Finally, you should study Peel's response to the infamous Irish famine of 1845–46.

Sir Robert Peel was considered to be an expert on Irish affairs, having served as Chief Secretary for Ireland between 1812 and 1818. Initially he had gained the reputation of being a hardline Protestant, determined to uphold the interests of the Anglican Church in Ireland, the Church of Ireland. So clear were his anti-Catholic feelings that he was given the nickname 'Orange Peel'. This stance won him many supporters within his own Tory Party, traditionally the party that supported the Church of England, which was strongly anti-Catholic. His connection with Irish affairs continued when he became Home Secretary under Liverpool and then Wellington.

Roman Catholic emancipation

In 1829 the Tory government faced a major crisis in Ireland, when demands for Roman Catholic emancipation were made. Catholics until that point had been denied political rights and were unable to sit as MPs in the British Parliament in London. The situation was far from satisfactory and the campaign for emancipation gained momentum under a Dublin lawyer, Daniel O'Connell. He was the leader of a non-violent movement known as the Catholic Association and was hugely popular among the people. In 1828 his opportunity came when a by-election occurred in County Clare. O'Connell put himself up for election knowing that he was sure of victory. He was duly elected MP for County Clare but was unable to represent his constituency. Ireland was seething with discontent and unrest, which would only stop if O'Connell could take up his seat. Wellington faced a major crisis, which could only be resolved if the law was changed and Roman Catholics were granted emancipation. Knowing how anti-Catholic the Tory Party and the House of Lords were, both Wellington and Peel faced a momentous decision. They decided that the law must be changed to avoid civil war and anarchy in Ireland. The **Emancipation Bill** was finally passed in April **1829** and O'Connell and other Catholics were allowed to enter the British Parliament on equal terms. Peel especially was heavily criticised by the Tory Ultras for what they considered a humiliating U-turn; he was determined not to be defeated by O'Connell again.

The defeat of the repeal movement

The two old enemies crossed swords again when Peel became Prime Minister in 1841. On this occasion the issue that separated the two men was the repeal (break-up) of the union between England and Ireland, signed in 1800. The Repeal Association, led by O'Connell, was determined to put the issue at the forefront of politics and convinced that a mass movement would force Peel to give in to public pressure once again. Peel, although facing serious internal problems from the Chartists (a working-class movement campaigning for voting rights), was quite prepared to use force to save the union. The crucial year was 1843, when a huge protest meeting was organised by the Repeal Association at Clontarf. Peel acted swiftly to ban the meeting and arrest

O'Connell. On this occasion Peel had kept his resolve and, deprived of its leader, the repeal movement quickly collapsed.

The issue of land

The whole episode with O'Connell and the repeal movement forced Peel to take a closer look at some of the grievances of the Irish people, in particular the issue of land tenure (the way in which land was held). In 1843 he appointed Lord Devon to investigate their grievances. He identified a number of problems:

- **Leases on lands were too short** and not expected to exceed three lives. There was therefore no incentive for Irish peasants to invest and make improvements and no compensation was given even if they did.
- **Evictions from the land were common** by the English (often absentee) landlords.
- **Rents were extremely high** as a result of a growing population. Many peasants were landless and forced to live on only potatoes.

When Devon reported his findings in 1843, he recommended limited compensation for those tenants who had carried out improvements on their land. Peel agreed and drew up a bill in support. The whole issue, however, was defeated by the Lords, who refused to improve the life of the Irish peasant.

Education policy

Having failed to deal with the issue of land, Peel now turned his attention to education. He was convinced that the role of the priesthood needed to be re-examined. Priests were such a crucial link between rulers and ruled and so influential in Irish life that Peel thought they should receive money to help win them over to the establishment. In 1845, £30,000 was to be given to the Irish College at Maynooth, an important institution in training Catholic priests. Despite the opposition of some 149 of his own party, the **Maynooth Grant** was passed. Public opinion in England was outraged that public money was being used to train the enemy. Peel was unmoved by the criticism and determined to win over the moderates and alienate the extremists. This was not done without the loss of one of his most loyal supporters, William Gladstone, who resigned in disgust at the grant.

Famine and its consequences

The most infamous piece of Irish history in this period was the Irish famine, between 1845 and 1849. Peel as Prime Minister was faced with a humanitarian catastrophe of the type we witness frequently today in Africa. The problem for Ireland was that its potato crop had failed on successive occasions and the poor were literally starving to death. Prices tended to increase in a crisis and there was no welfare state in existence to help. Peel had to do something to aid the poor and the quickest way of doing so would be to repeal the tariffs on all foodstuffs, including the celebrated **Corn Law** of 1815. This would bring in cheap food and, more importantly, save lives. Peel knew, however, that the majority landowning interest within his own party would find this

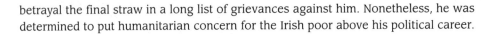

betrayal the final straw in a long list of grievances against him. Nonetheless, he was determined to put humanitarian concern for the Irish poor above his political career.

Conclusion

Ireland was important for Peel's career for a number of reasons:
- He had his first experience of Cabinet responsibility as Chief Secretary for Ireland from 1812 to 1818.
- He was arguably the first modern politician to grasp the complexities of Irish affairs as regards land, religion and education.
- He successfully resisted the repeal movement led by O'Connell.
- His Irish policies brought him into open conflict with critics within his party.

How effective was Peel as a party political leader?

Summary

Peel was leader of the Tory/Conservative Party from around 1830 up to his fall from office as Prime Minister in 1846. For this key issue you need to explore how well he led his party and how successfully he and his party adapted to the changing political circumstances of the 1830s and 1840s. You should focus on his response to the passage of the 1832 Reform Act and the importance of the Tamworth Manifesto in 1834, which some claim saw the birth of the modern Conservative Party. You will also need to be aware of the unpopularity of the changes Peel introduced within the party, the false promises he made during the 1841 election campaign and the splits in the party as a result of the repeal of the Corn Laws in 1846.

Party reorganisation

The passage of the **Reform Act in 1832** (which increased the number of people who could vote and forced both parties to organise themselves more effectively) had a fundamental impact on the development of politics in nineteenth-century Britain. The fact that the middle classes possessed the vote forced the two leading parties, the Whigs and the Tories, to alter their beliefs and policies to accommodate them. Peel, who became leader of the party after Wellington, opposed the changes of 1832 because he knew they would lead to more. He was quite convinced that the old system worked and saw no reason to alter it. Yet he was not going to stand still and watch events pass him by. He grudgingly accepted these new changes and, like a true politician, looked to remodel the party in order to react to them. The establishment of the Carlton Club in 1831 created a centre for the reorganisation for the party, and working out who was able to vote was now vital for electoral success. Peel was unpopular with many in his party over his policies on Ireland, but nobody doubted his impressive administrative ability and outstanding intellect. He was a brilliant speaker and in many ways the leading light in the party; and despite his northern industrialist background, he managed to lead a predominantly landowner-dominated party with a south-of-England bias. He was fortunate that during most of the 1830s he was out of office and thus able to bring about the changes in the party he wanted, without the pressure of government.

Tamworth Manifesto

In December 1834 Peel issued his famous Tamworth Manifesto, which modern historians agree saw the birth of the modern-day Conservative Party. Its aim, according to Peel, was to 'combine, with the firm maintenance of established rights, the correction of proven abuses, and the redress of real grievances'. In other words, Peel was aiming to combine traditional Tory values such as the maintenance of law and order with a wider appeal designed to win over the middle classes. It was a sensational piece of propaganda, aiming to 'turn the Tory Party of one particular class [the aristocracy] into the Conservative Party of the nation'. It was not popular with traditional Tory supporters, but the promising electoral gains made in 1835 and 1837 showed the message was beginning to win over the middle classes. Peel's profile was raised when he formed a minority government, 1834–35. However, he was forced to resign when a group of Irish radicals, led by O'Connor, combined with the Whigs to overthrow his administration.

The 1841 election

By 1841 Peel was convinced his new-look party was ready for government. The Whigs under Lord Melbourne had lost their cutting edge and were ripe for the taking. The result saw a comfortable victory and Peel was sworn in as Prime Minister with a majority of 76. What is interesting about the 1841 election is that Peel was returned on a pledge to retain the Corn Laws and made the greatest gains in traditional Tory seats. The mass exodus of the middle classes from the Whigs to the Conservatives, especially in the north, had not materialised and in many ways Peel had lied during the election campaign in order to return to office.

There is no doubt that Peel was now committed to many policies that would upset the landowning, Tory members of his party, as his ministry between 1841 and 1846 was to prove. He was always of the belief that the welfare of the nation was far more important than the narrow interests of his party. He was first and foremost the Queen's first minister, responsible for the nation's welfare; for Peel, leadership of the Conservative Party always came a very poor second. As the true nature of his arrogant leadership became apparent, critics within the party, such as the young Benjamin Disraeli, condemned Peel for ignoring the wishes of the parliamentary elite and setting his own political agenda. In many ways the crisis of 1845–46 in Ireland provided Peel with a convenient excuse to split the party. Once he had resigned from office, the old party split into Peelite and Tory factions. It was a major setback. The consequence for the party was 20 years out of office.

Conclusion

Peel's effectiveness as a party leader is a highly contentious topic. One could see it positively in that he:

- **reorganised the party** and adapted to the changes of 1832
- **widened the party's basis of support**, as shown in the Tamworth Manifesto of 1834
- **won the 1841 election** and returned the party to power
- **created the Carlton Club** and put the party on a national footing
- always pursued **Protestant policies in Ireland**

Equally, he can be criticised as a party leader for:

- **ignoring the wishes of the majority** of his party over major policy issues
- **lying to the electorate in the 1841 election**, claiming he was committed to retaining the Corn Laws
- **turning his back on the party**, when it had in many ways given him a chance to display his talents
- **splitting the party** over his actions during the repeal crisis of 1846, which condemned them to 20 years in opposition
- **putting the nation's interests first**, knowing that it would upset the majority interest within his own party

Why is Peel's ministry of 1841–46 considered to be so successful?

Summary

For this key issue you will need to study Peel's financial reforms, such as the introduction of income tax in 1842 and the reduction of tariffs, as well as the policies intended to win over the business community, such as the Bank Charter Act and the Companies Act. Peel's social reforms, such as the passage of the Factory Acts in 1842 and 1844, will also need to be covered.

Peel's financial policy

Arguably, Peel's ministry between 1841 and 1846 was the most successful of the whole century and it had a major impact, especially on the business community. Yet Peel could not have faced a worse situation when he took office in 1841. There was unrest in Ireland and the Whigs had left a budget deficit of over £2m. In addition, the working classes flocked to the Chartist movement, demanding the vote among other things. Peel's solution to these problems was a simple one, as he himself declared: 'We must make this country a cheap place to live in...enable the people to consume more by having more to spend.' The starting-point for prosperity was the 1842 budget, which Peel drew up personally.

The most sensational element of the 1842 budget was the **reintroduction of income tax**, at a rate of 7 pence in the pound on incomes over £150 per year. Despite the opposition of the majority of his party, the measure proved to be a spectacular success — the Whig deficit was overturned and a healthy surplus remained. No government has been able to do without it since.

The budget also saw the **lowering of tariffs**. Businessmen argued that tariffs (taxes on imports) were too high and made food far too expensive for the lower classes. In his budgets of 1842, 1843 and 1845 Peel swept away the duties on over 600 articles and the duties on over 500 others were severely reduced. For example, items such as raw cotton, meat and potatoes were now completely free from import duty. Peel argued that reduced tariffs would bring down the price of British goods abroad, increase exports, stimulate industry and provide jobs. These measures worked exactly as Peel hoped: trade revived, exports increased, unemployment fell and goods became cheaper.

Peel also reorganised the shaky financial structure he had inherited. In **1844** the **Bank Charter Act** was passed. This ensured that new banks were no longer allowed to issue notes, a practice which had led to several financial crises. The Bank of England was given control over banknote issues, which had to be linked to existing gold reserves and securities. This proved to be another success and the financial crises that were such a feature of the early nineteenth century disappeared. This measure could be seen as the starting-point for the modern methods used to control an economy. The **Companies Act (1844)** was also designed to improve business efficiency. Peel forced companies to register and produce annual accounts, ensuring more honesty in business and increasing taxation opportunities for the government.

Social policy

As described on page 22, Peel had passed a number of social reforms while he was Home Secretary under Liverpool. He had also seen the legislation passed by the Whigs during the 1830s and generally welcomed their humanitarian feeling. In **1842** he introduced the **Mines Act**, which forbade women and children under ten from working underground, and in **1844** the **Factory Act** was passed. This measure reduced the working hours for those under thirteen and recommended various safety improvements in factories, such as the fencing of machinery.

Conclusion

Peel's ministry was considered to be so successful for a variety of reasons:
- It dealt with **Chartist unrest** by improving living and working conditions, thus eliminating many of the grievances the Chartist movement used for support.
- It transformed the **condition of the working classes** through reduced tariffs and its positive consequences.
- The **financial structure** of the country was reorganised with the Bank Charter Act and the success of the various budgets.
- Businesses were placed on a more secure footing with the **Companies Act** of 1844.

- **Social improvements** took place in the mines and factories.
- There was an attempt to deal with **Irish issues**.
- The **Corn Laws were repealed** in 1846, bringing in a generation of prosperity.
- **Economic growth** accelerated, and the budget deficit inherited from the Whigs was turned into a healthy surplus.

Yet, as we have seen in studying the previous key issue, not everyone shared this view:
- The aristocratic opponents within Peel's party complained bitterly about the **reintroduction of income tax** and the reduction of tariffs.
- Opponents also complained about his **Irish policy**.
- They objected to Peel's **personal arrogance**.
- The reforms in the **mines and factories** could have gone further.
- It could be argued that it was the **railway boom** (and not Peel's reforms) that created mid-Victorian prosperity.
- The **repeal of the Corn Laws** split the party.

Why did Corn Law repeal lead to the collapse of Peel's government in 1846?

Summary

The repeal of the Corn Laws in 1846 was one of the most celebrated events of the nineteenth century and was welcomed by most of the middle and working classes. Yet it split the Conservative Party, led to the fall of Peel from office, and relegated the Conservatives to 20 years in opposition. The focus in this key issue is on how and why the repeal had such dramatic consequences. You will need to know why the adoption of free trade by Peel had such a dramatic impact on a predominantly protectionist party. You should also understand the influence of the Anti-Corn Law League as well as the circumstances and reasons for repeal in 1846.

The need for change

The Corn Law passed by Lord Liverpool in 1815 was intended to protect the agricultural community from ruin. Peel, however, despite campaigning for its retention in the 1841 election, had almost certainly decided that it would have to go at some point in the future. In 1842 there was a slight reduction in the import duty on corn, and the more successful his free-trade policies became, the more convinced Peel was that the Corn Laws were out of place in a newly industrialised Britain. He was also convinced by the arguments of the **Anti-Corn Law League**. This was a middle-class pressure group set up in 1838 by two Manchester industrialists, Richard Cobden and John Bright. They embarked on a spectacularly successful campaign. They gave lectures, started their own newspaper and used their influence in Parliament to bring the benefits of free trade to the forefront of people's minds.

The Irish famine provided Peel with the excuse he needed and he introduced a bill to repeal the Corn Laws in 1846; this was designed to phase them out over 3 years. Peel's justification was that retaining them was immoral and he appealed to his own party with the argument that its standing would improve if they agreed to a measure that was obviously beneficial to most people. His opponents, such as **Disraeli** and **Bentinck**, feared that the country would be flooded with cheap grain and that agricultural landowning interests would be ruined. Despite the fact that two-thirds of his party voted against him, the bill was passed with Whig support in June 1846. Ironically, it was another Irish issue that led to Peel's final defeat in the same year. He wanted to introduce a Coercion Bill to imprison anyone for as long as the government pleased to quell unrest in Ireland, but it was defeated. This forced Peel to resign as Prime Minister. Thus ended the career of one of Britain's greatest political leaders.

Conclusion

Why did Corn Law repeal lead to the collapse of Peel's government?
- He lost the support of two-thirds of his party.
- He had proved to be untrustworthy over the issue.
- He was regarded as being under the influence of the Anti-Corn Law League.
- The Irish famine provided a smokescreen for his true intentions.
- He genuinely believed in the positive consequences of free trade.
- The Whigs took advantage of the splits in Tory ranks over repeal and outvoted him over the Irish Coercion Bill.

The economy and industrialisation, 1780–1846

The four key issues for study and examination are:
(1) Why was Britain the first industrial nation?
(2) What was the nature and extent of change?
(3) Why were there so many problems in the countryside?
(4) What were the popular responses to economic change?

Why was Britain the first industrial nation?

Summary

The Industrial Revolution, which started in Britain in the late eighteenth century, is one of the most important events in history. The purpose of this key issue is to ask why Britain was the first nation to experience such a change in its economic make-up. In the course of this section candidates will need to define what is meant by industrialisation as well as studying the relative importance of population growth, overseas trade, new inventions, the geography of Britain, the availability of finance for investment and social changes in making Britain the first industrial nation.

The Industrial Revolution — a brief definition

Defining the 'Industrial Revolution' is notoriously difficult. The historian Anthony Wood described it as 'a momentous change from an agrarian to an industrial society'. While this may be a little simplistic, we need to emphasise at the outset that this was a huge turning point in human development. All historians now agree that industrialised societies are predominantly urban, have higher rates of economic growth, provide higher living standards and allow for more investment in industry.

Britain in the eighteenth century

Britain had already seen the beginnings of industrial growth in the eighteenth century, especially in the cotton industry. The country was becoming more urbanised and possessed all the advantages that were required for sustained economic growth when the opportunities arose:

- **Population growth:** this acted as a real catalyst for economic growth. Britain's population had been rising in the eighteenth century and had reached around 10.5 million by 1801. This number continued to grow as the Industrial Revolution developed, and had reached 14.1 million by 1821. A growing population was important for two main reasons:

  (1) It provided the extra workforce needed to fill the new factories.

  (2) It created a rising demand for industrial goods.

- **Growth in foreign trade:** the eighteenth century witnessed a steady growth in trading opportunities, especially with North and South America. Trade statistics show a remarkable growth in all areas, but especially in the textile industry, which accounted for two-fifths of all exports in 1810. The power of the navy certainly helped in this regard, and businesses and trading companies were desperate to take advantage of a larger foreign market by producing more goods at home. Trade with Europe also increased in the early part of the nineteenth century as the effects of the loss of the American colonies were felt. There were times, however, when foreign trade growth was uneven, especially as a result of the disruption caused by the Napoleonic Wars, but it is still a vitally important factor in the development of the Industrial Revolution.

- **High-profile inventors:** Britain was fortunate to have an extraordinary number of inventors during this period. In all areas of economic growth British inventors led the way. James Watt built the first steam engine in 1776, overcoming the problems of relying solely on water power. In 1709 Abraham Darby had discovered that coke could be used in the smelting of iron. By 1782 Darby's family had refined this process of iron smelting in the Coalbrookdale area of Shropshire and was well placed to take advantage of the opportunities offered by the Industrial Revolution. The textile industry was also fortunate to have men like John Kay, James Hargreaves, Samuel Crompton and Richard Arkwright. They ensured that Britain was at the forefront of technological change and enabled the larger factories to churn out mass-produced textiles for a global market. At the same time, Josiah Wedgwood enjoyed a worldwide reputation for the quality of his pottery.

- **Geographical advantages:** Britain had a number of navigable rivers, such as the Severn, making the inland transport of goods relatively easy, and access to the sea was never far away for export opportunities. Fast-flowing rivers aided water power and when steam took over, the rich coalfields of South Wales and the East Midlands powered the new inventions. The northwest also had an ideal climate for processing cotton, the damp atmosphere generally preventing the cotton thread from breaking during spinning. Britain's various geographical advantages worked well together, and the country was unique in this regard.
- **Risk capitalists:** in order to make money at this time, Britain needed a generation of risk capitalists who were willing to take a chance despite the risk of failure. Fortunately, this happened as middle-class factory owners reinvested their profits back into the workplace and ensured the profits were passed down to the next generation (for example, the Darby iron dynasty). Many of these captains of industry were nonconformists, persecuted by the state and denied opportunities in conventional careers. A successful business could also confer social status and some of these men made huge personal fortunes.
- **Agricultural change** was a key factor in the development of industrialisation. The enclosure of common land into fields, together with improved land use and productivity, meant that a growing population could be fed. Moreover, without the ability to grow more food using less labour, there would not have been a pool of surplus labour for the factories.

Conclusion

Britain was the first industrial nation because:

- a **rising population** throughout the period created the demand and the work-force
- **foreign and internal trade opportunities** increased as demand for British products escalated
- **British inventors** led the way and ensured that machinery was created which could keep up with demand
- **Britain's geographical diversity** gave it an in-built advantage over its competitors and allowed growth in any sector of the industrial economy
- **entrepreneurs** took huge risks in investing in these new industries but were sometimes well rewarded with increased social status and massive wealth
- **agricultural change** led to more food being grown and less hunger, with surplus labour being made available for the new factories

What was the nature and extent of change?

Summary

This key issue focuses on the extent of change as a result of the Industrial Revolution. You need to be aware of the mechanisation of machines (such as the Spinning Jenny and Crompton's Mule) and the rate of change in the workshops and factories. You should also study the development and extension of trading opportunities and the growing urbanisation of cities such as Leeds and Birmingham, both key centres of industrialisation. Finally, you should know about the massive changes in transport, affecting roads, canals and railways.

Factories

The development of workshops and factories with increased mechanisation ensured that the domestic industry of the pre-industrial era was gone for ever. These factories tended to be built near to centres of population, close to the source of their raw materials and with good transport links. Initially, conditions in the factories were very harsh, with poor housing and inadequate public health making matters worse for the people who had to produce the goods. Gradually, however, industrialists began to realise their responsibilities, improving the working conditions and building affordable housing near to their factories.

The transport revolution

The success of the industrialisation process was also heavily reliant on the transport revolution which took place at this time. First came the canals. The building of the Bridgewater canal in 1761, linking Worsley and Manchester, showed what could be achieved. It led to the building of an extensive canal network which linked the major industrial areas and ensured that goods were transported relatively cheaply. By 1820 over £20m had been invested and some 4,000 miles of canal built.

Road building also aided the growth of industrialisation. Men like Thomas Telford and John Loudon Macadam ensured that the quality of road building was much improved and that the country's major cities were linked.

Arguably the greatest transport development was the railway boom, which reached its peak in the 1840s. The pioneering work of George Stephenson in the 1820s in the northeast of England ensured that a steam-powered railway was one of the great successes of the Industrial Revolution. The **Railway Age**, as the period has been described, catapulted the Industrial Revolution onto another level. The demand for goods such as iron increased dramatically and the railways were able to soak up unemployment at a time when the Chartist threat was at its greatest.

Conclusion

Britain experienced an increased rate of change in industrialisation because of:

- the **growth of factories** in major cities, which increased output and productivity
- the development of a **canal network** for bulk transport, which largely took place between 1760 and 1820
- the building of **new and better roads** to link major cities
- the tremendous **growth of railways** and related industries, which reached a peak in the 1840s

Why were there so many problems in the countryside?

Summary

Although the Industrial Revolution strengthened Britain's economic position, it did not create much enthusiasm in the countryside. Many people were affected as a result of the enclosure movement, which improved soil cultivation and animal husbandry. The movement had dramatic consequences for struggling labourers, who were forced off their land. It brought seasonal employment during harvest time in the summer but created poverty throughout the year in many rural areas. It also had an effect on the local ratepayers as it led to an increased contribution towards the Poor Law — the only method of social welfare at this time. You should study the mechanisation of agriculture — the inventions of Jethro Tull and Robert Townshend — which accelerated change in the countryside.

The agricultural revolution

Throughout the eighteenth century the countryside experienced its own period of gradual change in what historians have termed the 'agricultural revolution'. From about 1760 to 1820, however, this took on a greater momentum. The **enclosure movement** was at the forefront of these changes and transformed the make-up of the rural economy. In the century after 1750, over 4,000 Acts of Parliament resulted in the enclosure of around 20% of the cultivatable land available in England and Wales. Most of the new area under cultivation was used to grow barley and wheat to help feed a growing population.

The enclosure movement encouraged landowners to take more care of their land and also had a number of other important consequences:

- **It encouraged the mechanisation of agriculture:** it helped to produce a generation of agricultural pioneers — Robert Bakewell improved livestock breeding; Viscount Townshend improved the use of land by developing crop rotation; and Jethro Tull introduced a new seed drill. Landowners were encouraged to drain their land more efficiently and experiment with different crops. Enclosure made the best use of thousands of acres of wasteland.
- **Farms became more profitable:** by 1800, for example, an enclosed farm was

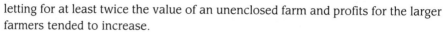

letting for at least twice the value of an unenclosed farm and profits for the larger farmers tended to increase.

- **Rural labourers were thrown off their land:** they were unable to contribute to the costs of enclosure and were forced to sell their strips of land and seek employment as hired labour.

Rural labourers

The massive agricultural changes brought little reward for the large number of labourers in rural areas at this time. From 1780 to 1850 the situation faced by the rural labourer was a very poor one. The growth in population did not help matters as wheat prices rose and wages dropped, and the rural labourer was forced either to head for the urbanised industrial areas where there was guaranteed factory employment or to stay in the countryside and fashion a miserable existence from the land. Most labourers chose the latter because they simply did not want to leave familiar surroundings and because poor relief would only be paid in the parish of birth. The poor rate — the amount paid by the ratepayers of each parish to care for their poor — rose by 400% between 1780 and 1820. Ratepayers complained about what they termed 'idle vagrants' and encouraged the Poor Law guardians and overseers to be a lot more exacting in the requirements for individual relief, which had a devastating impact on the impoverished labourer. The Church of England, which took a tithe (or a tenth) of each farmer's produce, was also blamed for forcing wages down and making the situation faced by the rural labourer far worse.

Individual farmers had no alternative but to cut costs. Regular employment was replaced by **seasonal work** or **employment by 'task'**. Particular times of the year associated with harvesting and haymaking were always times of plenty, where labourers could charge heavily for their labour, but generally the picture was a bleak one for the remainder of the year. Women and children, who had previously been employed by a farmer as domestic servants or dairymaids, were now discarded. Unfortunately, unless they were able to engage in other trades, the family was almost wholly reliant on the husband's meagre wage. Poverty was therefore a fact of life for the rural labourer as wages fell and rationalisation of agriculture occurred. Not surprisingly, many took the law into their own hands and rebelled.

Conclusion

There was a crisis in the countryside because of the following:

- The **enclosure movement** deprived poorer farmers of land and forced them to sell their produce at a lower price.
- There was an increase in the number of people receiving the **'poor rate'**, which angered ratepayers who had to make extra contributions.
- Farm costs were cut and full employment in the countryside gave way to **seasonal work**.
- The **ensuing hardship** affected family life, causing low self-esteem and finally fostering rebellion.

What were the popular responses to economic change?

Summary

The response of the people to these massive economic changes forms the core of this key issue. The middle class created by the Industrial Revolution provided future leaders. These men ruled over the oppressed masses, who were exploited by enclosure or undercut by the mass production of the new factory. After 1825 the period also saw the creation of the first modern trade unions, and the development of a radical movement that campaigned for respect and credibility. The movement sometimes took the law into its own hands; the Luddites, for example, smashed the machinery of the new factories in protest at the loss of their own domestic market. The influence of the famous Welsh factory owner Robert Owen is relevant here.

Workers' rights

For many, the changes brought about by the industrial and agricultural revolutions had negative, even devastating, consequences. Under the repressive policies of Pitt and Lord Liverpool (see pages 16–21), radical movements such as the Luddites emerged, campaigning desperately to retain their domestic market. Difficulties were faced at the same time by labourers in the countryside, who were to complain bitterly in the so-called **Swing Riots** of 1830–31. Industrialisation also created poor working conditions and unsatisfactory housing for those who had to work in the factories. They had little protection from their trade unions, which had been banned in 1799 by Pitt but restored by Peel in 1824. The unions did not really possess enough influence to sway the government, especially after the Amending Act of 1825 that effectively banned strikes.

There were some powerful individuals who rose above the repressive tactics of their contemporaries. The Welsh factory owner Robert Owen pioneered fair practice in the workplace at his Lanark factory. He argued that a contented workforce was a more productive one and also saw that his workers were well fed and housed. In the long term, working-class protest movements like Chartism were significant because most of their aims were eventually achieved and working people learnt how to organise themselves in a mass movement. However, the working classes did not really gain representation and respectability until the Labour Party emerged at the end of the century to represent their interests.

The middle classes had their own protest movement in the form of the Anti-Corn Law League. This was a pressure group established to campaign for repeal of the hated Corn Laws and to introduce free trade. It was based in Manchester and led by Richard Cobden and John Bright. It was successful in raising public awareness, but it was Sir Robert Peel who finally saw the need for change and it was his decision to repeal the Corn Laws in 1847.

Conclusion

The popular response to economic change can be summarised as:

- a series of **radical protest movements** such as Luddism, the March of the Blanketeers and the Peterloo Protest in 1819
- the **Swing Riots** in the southeast of England, which showed how unpopular government economic policy had become by 1830–31
- the growth of working-class organisations such as **Chartism,** which were committed to extending the vote, introducing the secret ballot and securing salaries for Members of Parliament
- the appearance of a successful middle-class movement, the **Anti-Corn Law League,** which was created to campaign on a single economic issue

Questions
&
Answers

This section of the book advises you on how to answer the two types of question (Section A and Section B) associated with this module. Sample answers are provided for each question, showing A-grade and C-grade responses. Examiner comments (preceded by the icon *e*) are given for each of the answers. They point out strengths and weaknesses and possible ways in which the answer could be improved.

Section A questions

Section A questions are marked out of 30 and test the key skill of **explanation**. For this you must have the ability to go deeper than merely describing events, as you were asked to do at GCSE. It relies on a good historical understanding of the key events and requires you to ask why and with what consequences an event happened. Aim to write about one side of paper for this section of the exam. Use clear and concise English and always remember to answer the question set. As the whole examination lasts 1 hour, remember to spend no more than 25 minutes on this part.

Types of question

Generally there are three types of question possible in Section A:
(1) Identify and explain two factors which....
(2) Explain the nature of an event.
(3) Explain....

They are more or less the same question, requiring you to explain the historical problem you are confronted with in the essay. The quality of your answer will depend on the detail you put into your response and the amount of explanation you give. Try to avoid mere description or narrative. C is the highest grade you will achieve if you rely on this type of response. The mark scheme used by examiners for A-grade and C-grade answers is outlined below.

Grade A (24–30 marks)

The response explains the key issues in the question convincingly and relevantly. The answer is successful in showing a high level of understanding. **The answer focuses on explanation rather than description or narrative.** The quality of historical knowledge supporting the explanation is sound and is communicated in a clear and effective manner. The answer is well organised. The writing shows accuracy in grammar, punctuation and spelling.

Grade C (18–20 marks)

The response explains most of the key issues in the question convincingly and relevantly. The answer is successful in its level of understanding. **The answer is more descriptive or narrative in approach but there is some analysis.** The quality of historical knowledge supporting the answer is mostly satisfactory and is communicated in an effective manner. The answer is mostly well organised. The writing generally shows accuracy in grammar, punctuation and spelling.

An A-grade response mostly explains events and uses analysis, whereas a C-grade response merely describes or narrates events without really getting to the heart of the question. This difference will become clearer when different examples are given.

The age of Pitt and Liverpool, 1783–1830

Identify and explain two factors which helped to strengthen the Tories' hold on power between 1783 and 1793.

■ ■ ■

A-grade answer to question 1

The Tory Party under William Pitt the Younger held power at this time and was strengthened in the exercise of its power by two main factors. First, throughout the period in question it enjoyed the support of King George III. This was primarily because he admired Pitt's leadership qualities but equally because he detested the Whigs and especially their leader, Charles James Fox. Second, the Tories were strengthened by the impact of the French Revolution on England. The outbreak of the revolution in France forced Pitt to be more aggressive toward the radicals, increased loyalist support for the king and exposed the divisions between his Whig opponents.

ℓ A good clear statement of intent in the introduction. This candidate clearly identifies the two areas she is going to explore and, more importantly, explains their importance on the Tory hold on power in this period. She could have given alternative reasons, such as the strength of Pitt's domestic reforms, but generally there is a clear understanding of where she is going. All she has to do now is expand the two points she has raised in her opening comments.

George III was arguably the most influential politician of this period and used various techniques to appoint the ministry he wanted in power. His use of patronage allowed talented politicians to emerge; he had personally appointed Pitt in 1783 and forced the Whig ministry of Fox and North to resign in the same year. He ensured that his supporters packed the House of Lords and paid influential backbenchers to support his policies and beliefs. He also had the important power of being able to call elections when he saw fit. For example, he delayed calling a general election until 1784 to allow Pitt to stabilise his support in the country. In the Tories he found a party which shared his view that the exercise of royal power was vital for the stability of the country, and he saw the potential Pitt had as a politician even at the tender age of 24, when he became Prime Minister. Upsetting this formidable monarch was not a wise thing to do, as Pitt found to his cost in 1801 when the two political allies fell out over Roman Catholic emancipation.

ℓ In this paragraph the candidate remains with the question. She identifies the King's role and illustrates the power he enjoyed, such as the possession of patronage and calling elections when it seemed his favourites needed help. She identifies the link between the

King and the Tory Party (although perhaps more could be made of this) and the personal qualities he admired in the Tory leader Pitt. Good, clear explanation is present throughout and she uses her awareness of the larger historical period by going beyond 1793, which is entirely relevant in this case. She is clearly focused and still on course for a good mark.

The outbreak of the French Revolution in 1789 also strengthened the Tory hold on power in this 10-year period. Pitt feared that the ideals of Liberty, Equality and Fraternity would spread across the Channel and undermine the whole basis of English society (as they had done in France). He took a very strong line against those radicals that openly supported the revolution and in response passed repressive legislation. In 1792 he supported the Royal Proclamations against Seditious Writings and in 1795 passed the Two Acts as well as suspending Habeas Corpus on two occasions. He was also strengthened in power as a result of the loyalist public reaction to the French Revolution. The execution of the French king in 1792 appalled most sectors of the English public and there were many anti-Jacobin riots in this period. The personal popularity of the King also rose substantially as a result. Finally, the French Revolution and its consequences fatally divided the opposition Whig Party. Two of its leading lights had a public disagreement over its merits. The Whig leader, Charles James Fox, embraced the revolution with open arms whilst Edmund Burke condemned it as being no better than anarchy in his influential book 'Reflections on the Revolution in France' published in 1790. In this situation, with his Whig opponents divided, Pitt and the Tory Party's hold on power was assured.

An excellent finishing paragraph, in which the candidate illustrates the effects of the French Revolution by citing Pitt's response as well as the division of the Whigs — two critical factors that strengthened the Tories' hold on power during this period. Again she shows good awareness of the wider picture, by crossing the 1793 dividing line to show examples of successful repressive legislation at the end of the period, which is entirely relevant to the question. The section on loyalist response clearly explains why the Tories became more popular and therefore strengthened their position. The complicated historical issue of the Whig divide over the French Revolution is simply explained and kept in the context of the question. Overall, this is a very good answer which would be awarded 26/30 marks.

■ ■ ■

C-grade answer to question 1

Pitt the younger was the youngest Prime Minister this country has ever had and he was to remain in office until 1803 before then returning to office briefly until his death in 1806. He was a skilled politician who was known for his knowledge of finance and administration. His career was varied and he enjoyed the support of King George III. He did not like the Whigs who he believed to be dangerous in their support of the French Revolution. He passed many policies in this period.

e This introduction lacks focus and is not specific enough to the question. We all know, for example, that Pitt was the youngest Prime Minister, but it does not have relevance to the question. The introduction should get to the point straightaway, and not waffle. There are too many generalised comments. There is also a factual inaccuracy: Pitt fell from office in 1801, not 1803.

Pitt was able to remain in office because of the strength of his policies. In 1784 he passed a Commutation Act designed to stop smuggling. In 1786 he signed the Eden Treaty with France. In 1784 he signed the India Act which gave the government a greater say in the running of this important colony. He also established the Sinking Fund designed to reduce government debt until the outbreak of war with France in 1794. He was very popular with the people, despite the fact that he increased indirect taxes on the rich, he taxed things such as windows and horses and other things as well.

e A good start here — Pitt's domestic reforms were a major reason why he stayed in power, but the reforms are simply listed in a narrative way, without explanation as to their importance in strengthening the Tories' hold on power. The knowledge displayed is good and accurate but of little value without explanation. Another factual error here: war broke out in 1793, not 1794.

He didn't like the whigs either and he hated their leader James Fox. He had little respect for Pitt and said that his ministry was like a bunch of mince pies not likely to last until Christmas. The whigs were also divided, which Pitt liked very much. They supported the French Revolution because it gave the people power and was a good thing to have. The whigs also lost the support of the King because they believed he was becoming too powerful and abusing his power over Parliament. If they didn't have the support of the King they wouldn't get into power because he was a very powerful man. All in all they stayed in power because Pitt had good policies and the opposition was divided.

e The candidate's use of English could be improved, such as using an upper-case 'W' for Whigs and writing 'Charles James Fox' in full. He demonstrates a rather simplistic understanding of the reasons why some (but not all) Whigs supported the French Revolution. He does, however, make a good point about the Whig fear of the excessive powers that the King enjoyed, but he should have related it to the question as set. Generally a disappointing answer, but there was lots of potential here if he had chosen to analyse and explain rather than describe events. His use of English would also be an area to work on, as would the inclusion of a little more detail. Overall, the answer would be awarded 18/30 marks, just scraping into the C grade.

The economy and industrialisation, 1780–1846

Explain the importance of two factors which were important for industrialisation in the period 1780–1846.

■ ■ ■

C-grade answer to question 2

Industrialisation is an important idea in this period. It occurred around the end of the eighteenth century and was important for a number of reasons. Firstly, it transformed the cities from rural areas into major industrial enterprises; it also ensured that businesses had to adapt to these new changes by building new factories in larger areas close to centres of population. It also led to the development of new inventions such as the Spinning Jenny and led to the emergence of major industrialists such as Josiah Wedgwood and Abraham Darby. Historians have found it very difficult to work out why it happened and there is still much controversy, which is still unresolved.

e There is some idea of the question here, but the introduction is rather rambling and lacks focus. The candidate makes the mistake of confusing the causes of industrialisation with the consequences and its significance. She would have been better employed in identifying two of the following possible factors — population growth, geographical diversity, the growth of foreign trade and new inventions — and developing them for the rest of the answer.

The growth in trade was a very important reason for the outbreak of the Industrial Revolution. The developments of overseas markets allowed British exporters to sell their new mass produced goods to a larger market and make bigger profits. This was especially true of the Iron Industry where the stimulus of war also aided this development. The navy was able to protect these interests and ensure Britannia ruled the waves. A growth in population also created the industrial revolution. This is because there were more mouths to feed, especially in the countryside. The population created a workforce to man these new factories and soak up the unemployment of the cities. Between 1801 and 1851 there was a massive population increase, but this also caused social problems in the cities and there were too many workers going for the same job, especially in the countryside. The geography of England was very important because there was coal to fuel the new steam engines, large navigable rivers to transport goods to and from industrial centres, and the correct climate to process raw cotton coming in from America. Businessmen were also willing to invest large amounts of money in the whole process, such as the Darby family of Coalbrookdale in Shropshire. They invested huge amounts of money in the new Iron industries and made substantial profits as a result. All in all, this was a very complex

question

process that changed the lives of people for ever. It could still be argued that it is having a huge impact on our lives today.

🖉 In this paragraph the candidate does manage to be more relevant and some good analysis emerges. She identifies the factors she missed in the introduction and uses some good knowledge to support her argument. Her major failing here, however, is that she tries to cover too many topics. Remember that the question only asks for two causes. If you try to cover everything, then the sharp focus you need to do well is lost. Perhaps a few points could have been developed and examined in a little more detail, but remember that you should only spend a maximum of 25 minutes on this section. This candidate does know the material, but the answer should have been a little more focused on the question set and she ought to have got to the heart of the issue more quickly. This answer would have been awarded a mark of 19/30.

Section B questions

This section is marked out of 60. A maximum of 15 marks is given for **perspective** and 45 for **evaluation**. You need to spend around 40 minutes answering this question and aim to write around two and a half to three sides. Refer to pp. 9–10 for advice on how to structure and answer an essay. Evaluation is obviously a very important ingredient in being successful on this paper. Put simply, evaluation is all about analysing and explaining rather than just describing historical events. Good use of perspective involves being able to give a wide-ranging answer that relates to the whole of the period required by the question. Examiners need to see that students understand the whole of the period and the issue they are dealing with. They do not expect total coverage, but equally they require a good understanding of the different arguments.

Types of question

There are a number of question types in Section B. They will all ask for an evaluation of the issue and in most cases ask you to answer for and against the question posed:
- How far did...?
- To what extent do you agree that...?
- Assess the view that...
- Compare the importance of at least three issues in...
- How effectively did...?
- How valid is the claim that...?
- Why did...?
- Why was...?
- '[a quotation]' How far do you agree with this point of view?
- How accurate is the view that...?

The quality of your answer will depend on how much factual detail you include as well as the amount of analysis you give. A-grade answers will be full and accurate, with a good understanding of the perspective indicated within the question. C-grade answers will still have to cover a fair amount of detail but perhaps will be a little too descriptive — although examiners will still expect a fair amount of analysis. The mark scheme (on the two areas of perspective and evaluation) used for A-grade and C-grade answers is outlined below.

Perspective: grade A (12–15 marks)

The response develops key issues about the perspective(s) in the question. **The answer is successful in showing a high level of understanding of the perspective.** The quality of recall, selection and accuracy of historical knowledge, applied relevantly to the perspective, is sound and is communicated in a clear and effective manner. The writing shows accuracy in grammar, punctuation and spelling.

Perspective: grade C (9–10 marks)

The response develops most key issues about the perspective(s) in the question. **The answer is mostly successful in showing a good level of understanding of the perspective.** The quality of recall, selection and accuracy of historical knowledge, applied relevantly to the perspective, is mostly sound and is communicated in a clear and effective manner. The organisation of the answer is uneven but there is a sustained argument. The writing generally shows accuracy in grammar, punctuation and spelling.

The key to a good mark on the perspective element of the paper lies in being able to develop the key themes or perspective contained in the question in a detailed and logical way. A C-grade response will fall down on its partial coverage and inadequate understanding of the perspective.

Evaluation: grade A (36–45 marks)

The response evaluates the key issues in the question convincingly and relevantly. The answer is successful in showing a high level of understanding. **The answer focuses on explanation rather than description or narrative.** The quality of historical knowledge supporting the evaluation is sound and is communicated in a clear and effective manner. The answer is well organised. The writing shows accuracy in grammar, punctuation and spelling.

Evaluation: grade C (27–30 marks)

The response evaluates most of the key issues in the question convincingly and relevantly. The answer is successful in its level of understanding. **The answer is more descriptive or narrative in approach but the evaluation depends on some analysis.** The quality of historical knowledge supporting the evaluation is mostly satisfactory and is communicated in an effective manner. The answer is mostly well organised. The writing generally shows accuracy in grammar, punctuation and spelling.

Clearly there is not much of a difference between the two grade descriptors. To gain a grade C you are still required to evaluate or analyse material. The higher-level response depends on the quality of your evaluation supported by detailed historical knowledge. This difference should become apparent in the two examples which follow.

War and peace, 1793–1841

Compare the importance of at least three issues which determined the conduct of British foreign policy in this period.

■ ■ ■

C-grade answer to question 1

There were a number of issues that determined the conduct of British foreign policy in the period 1793–1841. Each foreign secretary, regardless of their political background, was determined to uphold British interests as they defined them. They concentrated on the following, namely: strategic security, trade, the balance of power and naval power. They were in many respects linked together, especially the last two. It is very difficult to compare their importance, since contemporaries would have seen them as being equally important in the conduct of British foreign policy in this period.

e This is a decent if uninspiring introduction to the question. There is useful background knowledge and the candidate clearly identifies the interests he is about to discuss. He might have illuminated the introduction with examples to support each of these interests. He does at this point state that he is going to compare their importance and correctly states that they were all important in their own way. He evaluates, but so far there is no real attempt to put some perspective on the question with dates etc.

The importance of trade was undoubtedly a huge factor in the way in which British foreign secretaries operated in this period. The success of the Industrial Revolution created bigger export opportunities for business and it was the duty of the government to defend those interests. In 1793, for example, Britain declared war on France because France threatened British trading interests in Holland and the Low Countries. The loss of the American colonies in 1783 was also a stimulus to trade, as Britain was forced to look elsewhere and protect its interests in Canada (over which it still retained control). Castlereagh and Canning were particularly interested in protecting British interests in this area. The acquisition of naval bases such as Malta at the Treaty of Vienna in 1815 showed the importance of trade in this period. Palmerston was also determined that the USA did not break the promises it had made in 1807 to ensure that the slave trade was banned. The importance of trade was even more important in Britain's growing relationship with Turkey in the Near East. After the shock of the Treaty of Unkiar Skelessi in 1833, Britain decided on a more formal relationship with Turkey, especially for trading reasons. This would grow, as British interests were threatened by Russian designs in the area and ultimately led to war in the Crimea in 1854. Palmerston was also keen to safeguard the position of British trade in his dealings with the Chinese. Control and access to the lucrative opium market was the major reason for the outbreak of war between the two countries in 1839. The Treaty of Nanking that ended the war in 1842 was a success for Palmerston and showed the importance of trade to British foreign policy.

e This is generally a good paragraph with sound evaluation of the interests the candidate is discussing. The outbreak of war with France is well related to the issue of trade, as are developments at the Treaty of Vienna. He could have developed the issues relating to Canada and the USA by stating how they formed part of Canning's strategy to move away from a European dimension to Britain's foreign policy at this time. The section on Palmerston is comprehensive, but again he could have developed policy towards Russia a little more and revealed more of what he knew about Unkiar Skelessi. The material on China is also comprehensive and well incorporated into the answer. Up to this point there has been no real attempt to compare the importance of interests. It seems that the candidate is going for an approach whereby each interest is dealt with and then compared in the conclusion. It is better to integrate comparison and link interests together throughout. This approach is not wrong, but higher-level evaluation derives from the integrated approach. The perspective is good in this paragraph, however, and the whole range of the period is covered.

The balance of power was also an interest that concerned Britain in this period. The outbreak of war with France and the extent of Napoleon's empire by 1806 were of great concern to Britain and its allies. This concept was all about ensuring that no one country dominated at the expense of another. The peacemakers at the Treaty of Vienna in 1815 were determined that France would never again be in a position to threaten and invade countries. Yet for Britain, the greatest threat to the balance of power throughout this period was Russia. During the 1820s Canning was determined not to allow Russia to intervene on its own in support of the Greek Revolt, knowing how important Turkey was to Britain's trading and strategic position in the area. This hostility between the two countries continued under Palmerston in the two Near Eastern crises which occurred between 1831–33 and 1839–41. The success of the Straits Convention in 1841 ensured that the balance of power was maintained in the area at least for the immediate future.

e The issue of the balance of power is effectively analysed in this paragraph, but again comparison of interest and factual development are missing for a higher mark. The reader is also left frustrated by lack of detail in the reference to Russia. What was at issue for Britain in these crises needs clarification, and an explanation of the vital Straits Convention of 1841 is required. The candidate might have mentioned Palmerston's subtle diplomacy in this regard. Again, the comparison the examiner is looking for is absent in this paragraph.

The use of sea power was also very important in this period and was combined with the desire to maximise Britain's trading opportunities. The use of sea power was one of the main reasons why Britain was successful during the Napoleonic Wars. The success of Nelson at Trafalgar in 1805 was one of the major turning points of the war, for example. Napoleon's attempt to starve Britain was countered by the navy, which ensured that regular supplies reached the island. The importance of naval bases has already been mentioned and they were used to extend the empire further, for example the Cape of Good Hope acted as an incentive to move inland in South Africa.

The navy was used to search American slave ships and was used to bomb Alexandria in 1840 during the second Near Eastern crisis. Palmerston was clever enough to use the navy against the Chinese in the Opium War to devastating success.

e This is a rather brief paragraph on a rather important issue and one where the candidate could have linked it with and compared it to the importance of trade. Instead, he describes the events as he identifies them. Although Nelson is mentioned, the candidate could have developed the importance of the navy in saving Britain. There was also an opportunity to show the lengths Britain was prepared to go to in order to enforce its right to search slave ships and the problems it created in relations with the USA. The important Opium War is given cursory treatment here and the importance of the navy is hardly addressed at all.

Thus all these issues were important. Trade developed throughout the period and was used to further Britain's respectability. Britannia really did rule the waves at this point in history. Sea power was vital in the success of the Napoleonic Wars and ensured that Britain was safe from invasion and certain defeat. The balance of power was also very important because Britain feared the expansion of Russian influence and was prepared to fight to ensure it was repelled, especially in the Near East.

e This is a really disappointing conclusion and leaves the reader very frustrated. There is nothing new or original in it and it is basically a rerun of the introduction. The long-awaited comparison of the different interests does not materialise at all. The candidate therefore largely misses the point here. What examiners are looking for is a comparison of the interests mentioned in the question, with perhaps a conclusion as to which was the most important and why. The answer would have been awarded 9 marks for perspective and 29 marks for evaluation, making a total of 38/60.

The age of Peel, 1829–46

Assess the problems Ireland caused for Tory governments between 1829 and 1846.

■ ■ ■

A-grade answer to question 2

The act of Union in 1800 established Irish parliamentary union with Britain and contemporaries saw this as both a benefit and a disadvantage. Britain benefited from the increased taxes and English Protestant landlords, who were often absentee, held land in Ireland. The major problem was that there were religious tensions with the majority Catholic population, who resented paying tithes to support the Church of Ireland, and land-starved peasants, who were often discontented. In 1829 the issue of Roman Catholic emancipation divided the Tory Party and made its fall from power in 1830 inevitable. In 1834, under Peel's minority government, Irish problems also provided the Whigs with an opportunity to bring down the government with the Lichfield House Compact. Between 1841 and 1846 Irish affairs continued to cause problems for the government, and Peel's attempts to improve conditions in Ireland met with strong opposition. The deadly potato famine of 1845 was Peel's excuse for repealing the Corn Laws a year later and with it came a fall from power. The religious and political unrest in Ireland proved troublesome for the Tories and contributed to their fall from power on several occasions because of the strong emotions the issue provoked.

> *e* A good introduction: the problems are clearly identified and there is a sense of purpose and rigour in the argument. The candidate understands the problems associated with absentee English landlords and religious tensions caused by the payment of a tithe to the Protestant Church, to which few Irish people belonged. She also deals effectively with the difficulties associated with Catholic emancipation in 1829 and the splits it caused within the Tory Party. Unusually for a student of this period, she mentions the Lichfield House Compact that led to the fall of Peel's minority government between 1834 and 1835. The problems associated with the 1845 famine have been well understood, but perhaps some mention of the controversial Maynooth Grant in the same year might have improved this very encouraging start.

In 1829 Catholics had the vote if they had enough land, but could not hold public office, meaning they had little opportunity to change the existing situation. Since the Act of Union in 1800 there had been frequent violence that had been suppressed, but little had been done to tackle the causes of discontent. In May 1828, Daniel O'Connell, an Irish Catholic barrister, was elected by a large majority to the County Clare constituency, but could not take his seat. The Tory administration of Wellington faced a civil war in Ireland unless emancipation was granted. However, a large majority of the Tory Party opposed making concessions. In February 1829, Wellington and Peel, who everyone regarded as hard-line Tory Protestants, decided to support emancipation to prevent civil war, but in doing this made a U-turn and outraged Tory Ultras, leaving them determined to discredit the ministry. The Ultras were converted to the idea of electoral reform because they believed that a wider franchise would have rejected emancipation, and the issue drove them closer to the Whig opposition. The issue of emancipation therefore, and the consequences it aroused, left the Tory Party divided and weak and made electoral defeat in 1830 inevitable when the Ultras split away and supported Whig demands for electoral reform.

e A strong paragraph, perhaps a little too chronological, but there is enough evaluation present to impress. The consequences of emancipation are understood and the idea that the Tory Ultras were driven into supporting electoral reform comes over well. Ireland, in this instance, was clearly a thorn in the side of Wellington's administration and an important reason for electoral defeat in 1830.

In November 1830 Earl Grey became Prime Minister and passed the 1832 Reform Act as well as other important reforms. In 1834 unrest in Ireland led to a dispute over a Coercion Act that finally forced Grey to resign. A minority Tory/Conservative ministry led by Peel came to power but only for a hundred days. Lord Melbourne, the new Whig leader, realised that he could bring down the Tory government by cooperating with O'Connell and the Irish radicals. In February 1835 he agreed the Lichfield House Compact which gave them a majority over a government that was already a minority administration. Peel resigned in 1835 after several defeats in parliament. Ireland had caused problems for the Tories again and led to the end of Peel's government, but had not on this occasion split the party.

e Although Grey and the Whig reforms were not technically within the terms of the question, the candidate manages to mould the material eventually to make it relevant. The important Lichfield House Compact of 1835, where O'Connell's fledgling Irish Party supported the new Whig ministry of Lord Melbourne and kept the Tories out of office until 1841, is clearly another Irish problem the Tories failed to resolve.

In August 1841 the Tories returned to power with Peel as their leader for a second term of office. The party had become more conservative and changes, based on the 1834 Tamworth Manifesto, had been made, but Peel was aware that Ireland would still pose a problem. His policy in Ireland between 1841 and 1846 aimed to win over moderate Catholic support whilst keeping the key features of the Protestant establishment, a very difficult balance to strike. In 1843 O'Connell organised a meeting at Clontarf to highlight the demand of the Repeal Association, namely to end the union with Britain. Peel banned the meeting and passed a Coercion Act, and O'Connell was arrested, but Peel resolved to investigate how to improve relations with the Irish. In 1843 the Devon Commission investigated land tenure and recognised that peasants held short leases and could not be compensated if they invested in land during the lease, and that population growth and agricultural depression were making the situation worse. The commission recommended limited compensation for those tenants who invested, but this was very unpopular with Tory landlords in the party and the plan was defeated in the Lords. The appointment of the more liberal and pro-Irish Lord Heytesbury as Lord Lieutenant of Ireland in 1844 confirmed Peel's commitment to change, but he was unable to make any significant impact against the establishment view.

e A clear paragraph with strong evaluation of a key issue facing Peel's ministry between 1841 and 1846: namely, the problems caused by O'Connell's repeal movement in Ireland. The candidate clearly understands the material and shows a good command of perspective in showing how Peel dealt with the issue of land, such as the Devon Commission's moderate recommendations, which were thwarted by the landowners in the House of Lords.

Peel tried to fashion the understanding he envisaged between Catholics and Protestants through an attempt to remodel the education system. In 1844 he proposed the establishment of three non-sectarian Queen's Colleges in Ireland. The Tory Ultras and Catholics, sceptical about their 'godlessness', opposed the proposition. They were created, but the potential for conflict within the Tory Party was to surface sooner than expected. In 1845 Peel tried to gain the loyalty of the Catholic clergy, who were important political spokesmen, by offering to develop Maynooth College (which trained the priests) by offering £30,000 and an increased annual grant. Peel hoped that the priesthood would educate the peasants to accept his views, but 149 Tory backbenchers revolted against the Maynooth Grant and one of Peel's staunchest supporters, William Gladstone, resigned his Cabinet position as President of the Board of Trade. There was a hostile response in England, and Peel was seen to have betrayed the party and threatened the basis of Anglican control in Ireland.

e The continual problem of education is the subject of this paragraph. The candidate deals effectively with the Irish Colleges Bill of 1844 and notes the misgivings Peel still had to overcome on both sides. The training of Catholic priests at Maynooth is also given prominence and a clear evaluation of the problem emerges. Perhaps a little more is needed on the question of Peel's motivation, which would have strengthened the argument, but she is clearly in command of the material here.

The situation in Ireland had already caused serious problems for the Tories and tensions were running high, with Peel being accused of betraying the party. The situation worsened in 1845 when successive potato failures left peasants in Ireland starving and the system of relief unable to cope. Peel tactically used the situation as an excuse to repeal the Corn Laws. He believed that the only way to end the famine was by feeding Irish peasants with cheap grain from abroad. The Tory landlords, who feared ruin as a result of cheap grain flooding into Britain from abroad, saw the repeal as the ultimate act of betrayal. Finally, it was defeat over an Irish issue that led to his resignation in 1846. A combination of Whigs and Tory opponents voted Peel out over a Coercion Bill. It was ironic that once again Ireland came back to haunt Peel and end his career.

e The vital impact of the Irish famine of 1845 and the problems it aroused are dealt with in a sympathetic way here. What is especially impressive is the way in which the candidate manages to mould the Irish situation into the English context and show how the events in Ireland provided Peel with the excuse he required to repeal the Corn Laws. The consequences of repeal are also discussed in a mature manner and the main body of the essay ends on a perceptive note.

Thus Ireland caused numerous problems for Tory governments in this period, mainly because of the religious and land controversies it raised. The Tory Party was in a period of transition, from a party dominated by the agricultural landowning interest to one that appealed to the middle classes and was more broadly conservative in appeal. Problems in Ireland merely emphasised these divisions. Problems in Ireland were partly responsible for the collapse of all Tory ministries in this period, proving how influential Irish issues were on English politics and the fate of the Tory Party.

e The conclusion is a little disappointing as it could be interpreted as a reworking of the introduction. Perhaps the candidate would have been better employed identifying which was the most important Irish problem and why it proved so difficult to solve. Yet, overall, this is an impressive answer which identifies a range of problems affecting Tory policy in Ireland and has a clear command of two vital components of the new OCR specification: namely, an ability to evaluate — not just describe — events, and an understanding of the perspective of the question, going right through from 1829 to 1846. This answer would have been awarded a mark of 13 for perspective and 39 for evaluation, making a total of 52/60.